SONGS OF THE ISLAND

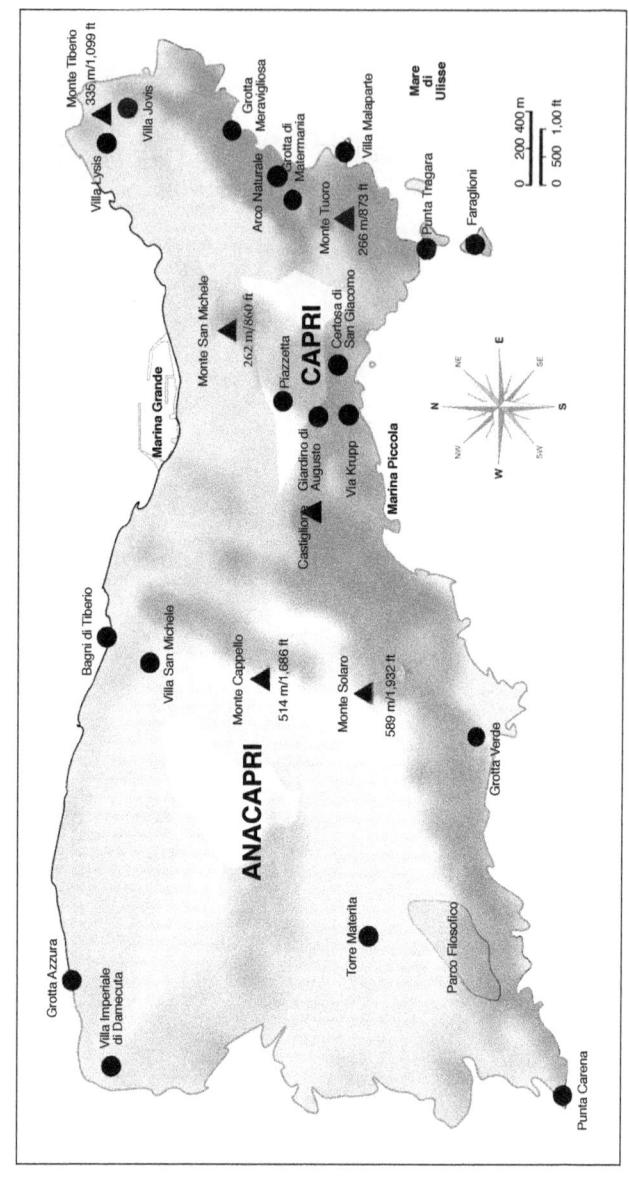

Songs of the Island

BY
Ada Negri

Translated by
Maria A. Costantini

Italica Press
New York
2011

Copyright © 2011 by Maria A. Costantini

ITALICA PRESS, INC.
595 Main Street, Suite 605
New York, New York 10044

All rights reserved. No part of this publication may be reproduced, stored in a retrieval system, or transmitted, in any form or by any means, electronic, mechanical, photocopying, recording, or otherwise, without prior permission of Italica Press. For permission to reproduce selected portions for courses, please contact the Press at inquiries@italicapress.com.

Library of Congress Cataloging-in-Publication Data
Negri, Ada, 1870–1945.
 [Canti dell'isola. English & Italian]
 Songs of the island / by Ada Negri ; translated by Maria A. Costantini.
  p. cm.
 English and Italian.
 Includes bibliographical references and index.
 Summary: "The first English translation of Negri's 1925 volume of poetry "I canti dell'isola," presented in a dual-language, Italian-English edition, with introduction, bibliography and first-line index. From the highpoint of her career, this work, based on her experience of Capri, explores the physical and spiritual experience of place"--Provided by publisher.
 ISBN 978-1-59910-207-8 ((hardcover : alk. paper) --
 ISBN 978-1-59910-166-8 (pbk. : alk. paper) --
 ISBN 978-1-59910-194-1 (ebk.)
 I. Costantini, Maria A., 1944- II. Title.
 PQ4831.E4C24513 2010
 851'.912--dc22

2010041538

Cover: View of Capri toward the Amalfi Coast. Italica Press Archives.
Map, p. ii: Based on map provided by Morn the Gorm, Wikimedia.

For a Complete List of
Italica Poetry in Translation
Visit our Web Site at
www.ItalicaPress.com

About the Translator

Maria Anna Recchia Costantini was born in the town of Casalvieri, near Rome, Italy, and came to the United States at age twelve. Her work in poetry and prose has the flavor of her Italian heritage and her immigrant experience. It has appeared in literary magazines and anthologies in print and online, and has won prizes and honors in contests by the National Federation of Poetry Societies, the Michigan Poetry Society, William Allen Creative Nonfiction, and Springfed Arts/Metro Detroit Writers. She is affiliated with Springfed Arts/Metro Detroit Writers, the Michigan Poetry Society, and the Dante Alighieri Society.

In late 2006, Costantini began to translate the poetry of Ada Negri, including the Italica Press editions of her translations of *Il Libro di Mara (The Book of Mara)* and *I Canti dell'Isola (Songs of the Island)*. She is currently working on the translation of *Maternità (Motherhood)*, Negri's third book of poetry (1904), as well as two personal projects: a collection of poems and a memoir. Formerly, Maria Costantini worked for twenty-eight years as a Bilingual/English-as-a-Second-Language teacher and chairperson in the Utica Community Schools. She has two grown children and resides in Rochester, Michigan, with her husband Franco.

To my husband Franco

Passo passo, m'accompagni lungo
  i giardini dell'Isola...."

Step by step, you accompany me
  along the gardens of the Island....

Fiori, Soavi Fiori /Flowers, Gentle Flowers,
by Ada Negri

Contents

MAP	II
INTRODUCTION	XI
GLOSSARY/ANNOTATIONS	XXIII
BIBLIOGRAPHY	XXVII

Songs of the Island

SOLARIA

Il male azzurro	2
The Blue Curse	3
L'offerta delle rose	4
An Offer of Roses	5
Notte di Capri	6
Capri Night	7
Il pergolato di glicini	8
The Wisteria Trellis	9
La cintura di giada	10
The Belt of Jade	11
Stanchezza	12
Fatigue	13
Sangue	14
Blood	15
La nave	16
The Ship	17
Vertigine	18
Vertigo	19
La luna scende in giardino	20
The Moon Descends on the Garden	21

COROLLE — COROLLAS

Rifugio fiorito	22
Refuge in Bloom	23
Per la tomba	24
For the Tomb	25
Fiori, soavi fiori	26
Flowers, Gentle Flowers	27
Euforbia	28
Euphorbia	29

Viola e nero	30
Violet and Black	31
Le tre corone	32
The Three Crowns	33
Benedizione	34
Benediction	35

L'UOMO E LA CASA — THE MAN AND THE HOUSE

L'uomo e la casa	36
The Man and the House	37
La Casa Solitaria	40
Casa Solitaria	41
Il Rosaio	42
Rosaio	43

CANZONI DELL'ALBA — SONGS OF DAWN

Mattutino	44
Matins	45
Colloquio	46
Conversation	47
Addio della luna	48
The Moon's Goodbye	49
Ancora un giorno	50
One More Day	51
La rugiada	52
The Dew	53
La grande stella	54
The Great Star	55

MIRAGGI — MIRAGES

Il segreto	56
The Secret	57
Filastrocca	58
Nursery Rhyme	59
La tessitrice	60
The Weaver	61
Miraggi	62
Mirages	63
La roccia	64
The Rock	65
La spiaggia delle vedove	66
The Widows' Beach	67
Torre Saracena	70
Saracen Tower	71

Scirocco	72
Sirocco	73
Maestrale	74
Mistral	75

Ulivi — Olive Trees

La sofferenza	76
Suffering	77
L'uliveto	78
The Olive Grove	79
Il paese	82
The Village	83

Nostalgie — Nostalgia

Casa Dòmina	84
Casa Dòmina	85
Lettera a Bianca	88
Letter to Bianca	89
Lettera a Bianca	92
Letter to Bianca	93
Le Strade	96
The Roads	97
Canzone bretone	98
Breton Song	99
Ritorno per il dolce Natale	100
Return for Sweet Christmas	101
Donata	104
Donata	105
Il sagrato	106
The Churchyard	107
Lontano	108
Away	109
Il mandorlo	110
The Almond Tree	111
Un sogno	112
A Dream	113
I capelli	116
Your Hair	117
La fronte	118
Your Brow	119

NEL PAESE DI MIA MADRE — IN THE VILLAGE OF MY MOTHER
   Nel paese di mia madre   120
      In the Village of my Mother   121
   Corale notturno   124
      Night Chorus   125

FIRST LINE INDEX   127

Introduction

la magia del sensibile e i baleni della invisibile realtà
— Vincenzo Schilirò

I. Songs of the Island

Toward the end of March 1923, Ada Negri enjoyed a brief holiday in Sicily and from there she went to the island of Capri, where she stayed for about a year. In Capri, she had the illusion of having discovered an earthly paradise and of having found the answer to her internal conflicts. There, she felt reborn and, in the process of writing *I canti dell'isola/ Songs of the Island,* her soul became exalted.

Her lyrics of Capri, full of sun, blueness and the perfume of oriental roses, are like a seashell: magical, polyphonic in their infinite melodiousness. Dedicated to the memory of Cesare Sarfatti, husband of Negri's best friend and fellow-writer Margherita Sarfatti, and that of their war-hero son Roberto Sarfatti, *I canti*'s poems represent a sort of parenthesis in Negri's work. They are the result of the blinding light of the island, the ardor of a holiday both physical and spiritual. In the words of Schilirò, they embody "the magic of the tangible and the flashes of invisible reality," and symbolize the poet's hour of quiet and reflection on her path thus far.[1]

The opening poem, *Il male azzurro/The Blue Curse,* introduces the reader to Negri's thematic dualities of love/ death, beauty/suffering, ecstasy/torment, thus setting the contrapuntal tone of the poems that follow. In these verses, the poet addresses the island's power over her, which brings her to the brink of insanity, and the treacherous blue lizard that exists only along the jutting rocks of the *Faraglioni* she refers to as Cyclops — perpetual guardians of the island.

---

1. Vincenzo Schilirò, *L'Itinerario Spirituale di Ada Negri* (Milan: Istituto Propaganda Libraria, 1938), pp.17–18. Web. Retrieved 1/8/2010, http://www.bronteinsieme.it

There's energy and languor in: *Ho male di luce, ho male di te, Capri solare*/Light pains me; you pain me, luminous Capri....

> Guizza ancor lungo i fianchi dei tre Ciclopi,
>   e sfavilla
> la lucertola azzurra che nacque al tuo nascere,
>   o Capri.
> ...Perfida come l'acqua che intorno agli scogli
>   in cristalli
> multisplendenti s'indura...
> Azzurra è la tua follia, Capri, nube del mare...
> S'io debba morire di te, dammi la morte azzurra.

Still darting alongside the three Cyclops,
    and sparkling,
is the blue she-lizard born at your birth,
    o Capri.
...Treacherous as the water that hardens around cliffs
    in glittering crystals...
Blue is your folly, Capri, cloud of the sea...
Should I die of you, grant me a blue death.

Via the impressionistic sweep of these images, we too are transported by Capri's explosion of light and color, its offering of "a thousand hearts for a thousand loves." Enchanted by pearls, amethyst and jade, the mythological sea of Ulysses, the unstoppable bleeding of poppies, *Il Rosaio's* climbing purple roses, *Casa Dòmina's* castaways of dreams, we want to be seduced, if only for a moment, by this world of the senses.

Yet, as if fraught with guilt, the human spirit aspires to a higher self. Note the following lines from *Le strade*/The Roads (1923), the prose counterpart of *I canti*:

> Dovrò pur salire gli scalini, arrivare fino a lassù, toccar con le mani la nube che s'affaccia a mezzo dell'arco. Nessun è con me: non vi sono appoggi: non vi sono che le due muraglie scabre: non v'è che questo candore.

> *Quando sarò là in cima troverò Dio. Povera è la scala; e non la salgono, io ne sono certa, che piedi scalzi o difesi da umili suole di corda. Anch'io sono povera: povera di tutto: non ho chi mi ami, nè chi mi protegga: se non mi guadagno la mia giornata, non ho di che vivere. La scala è adatta ai miei piedi; ed io la salirò così divotamente, che Dio non mi respingerà.* (Mondadori 1926, p.15)

> I shall indeed climb these steps, all the way to the top; with my hands touch the cloud that peeks in through the center of the arc. No one is with me: there are no supports: there is nothing but rugged walls: there is nothing but this whiteness. When I am at the top, I will find God. The staircase is poor: no one climbs it, I'm certain, but they whose feet are either bare or protected by humble soles of twine. I, too, am poor: poor in everything: with no one to love me, or protect me: if I don't earn my bread, I have nothing to live on. The stairs suit my feet; and I shall climb them so devoutly that God will not push me away.

A similar dichotomy of desire, of spirit versus flesh, recurs in *I canti*'s *Torre Saracena/Saracen Tower*, where the stairway to Saracen Tower is high, and "the ancient sea of castaways sings and shatters with love" against it, but the stairway listens only to "divine words from the sky." Also leading to heaven, in *La luna scende in giardino/The Moon Descends on the Garden*, a white road is born on the sea "for those who wish to reach God's palace in the night." Only, here, the poet chooses to stay in the garden and play with moon rays and shadows, in the gaze of her lover's "wide tranquil eyes" next to the moon.

II. Ada Negri's Road

At the turn of the twentieth century, much was being written about the young Italian poet. In its November 1900 issue, the *Philadelphia Conservator* published an English translation of *I vinti/The Defeated*, from Negri's first book of poems, *Fatalità/Fate (1892)*:

> And we sought faith that to ideals cleaves,
> Alas! we were betrayed;
> And we sought love that hopes and that believes,
> Alas! we were betrayed.
> And work we sought that gives new life and strength,
> Only repelled to be.
> Where then is hope? Oh mercy! Where is strength?
> The world's defeated, we!

Such verses cry out for revolution against all the wrongs and inequities of the world. Because of them, Negri, a village schoolmistress, became known as the champion of the masses. The slight, pale girl, with dark hair and beautiful eyes, became the prophetess of scenes of violence, bloodshed and martial law, which had actually come to pass not many years before in the streets of Milan.

Born on February 3, 1870, in the town of Lodi, near Milan, Negri spent her early years in the porter's lodge of a palace where her grandmother, Peppina Panni, worked as custodian and governess to the famous Milanese soprano Giuditta Grisi, wife of Count Barni. Young Ada spent the hours observing passersby, an experience she would later describe in her autobiographical novel, *Stella mattutina/ Morning Star* (1921). First-hand, she learned of the plight of the working class by observing her father Giuseppe, a manual laborer who died when she was small, and her widowed mother, Vittoria Cornalba, a weaver who slaved in a factory at starvation wages to earn bread for her child. And, "from all its pent-up bitterness, the tragedy of her sunless childhood broke forth with piercing pathos in her early works."[2]

---

2. Beatrice Marshall, "Ada Negri," *The Academy* (London, Publishing Office 43) 59 (July 1900): 521–25. Web: Retrieved 12/2009. http://www. books.google.com.

At eighteen, Negri left the damp hovel of her childhood to take a position as an elementary-school teacher in Motta-Visconti, a rural Lombard town. Meanwhile, as she began to publish her poems in popular newspapers, she gained people's interest.

In 1894, after the publication of *Fatalità*, Negri won the Milli Prize for poetry, which provided her with a small stipend and freed her to devote her time to writing. In 1895, she published *Tempeste/Tempests*, where she continued to pursue the theme of social injustice. Again, the poet "sings not of roses, nightingales, and moonlit gardens, but of the wrongs of humanity, gnawing hunger, grinding poverty," and lack of care.[3]

In 1896, she married industrialist Giovanni Garlanda, who fell in love with her just from reading her poetry, and by whom she had daughters Bianca in 1898 and Vittoria in 1900. The latter died in infancy. The marriage didn't last and, in 1913, Negri made her final separation from her husband by moving to Switzerland with Bianca. While there, she wrote *Esilio/Exile*, a book that gave voice to her personal conflicts as well as her dread of the imminent world war. After she re-entered Italy, she had a tormented love affair, the experience she described in *Il libro di Mara/The Book of Mara* (1919).

Ada Negri received the Mussolini Prize in 1931 and became the first woman to be admitted into the Royal Academy of Italy in 1940. It is possible that Mussolini's choice was influenced by a recommendation from the princesses of Savoy, who appreciated Negri's work. The Academy, founded in 1926 by Mussolini, was to:

> promote and coordinate Italian intellectual activity in the sciences, the humanities, and the arts, preserve the integrity of the national spirit according to the genius and tradition of the race, and encourage their

---

3. Idem.

diffusion abroad. It also served to strengthen the Fascist regime's hold on intellectual activity in Italy, as it demanded that all its members swear loyalty to Fascism and Italy.[4]

In 1943, in an attempt to escape the horrors of the Second World War, Negri moved to her daughter's home in Bollate, near Milan. But, from there, she could still hear the constant bombings on Milan. She moved farther: first to Gajone, then Pavia, to no avail. The war brought on such anguish in her that she requested her final work, *Fons amoris*, be published only after the war had ended. By 1944, still unable to find the peace she sought, Negri returned to Milan. On January 11, 1945, her daughter Bianca found her dead in her studio.

III. Overview and Early Criticism of Ada Negri's Poetry

Negri's poetic work evolves in three different phases: the first, comprised of *Fatalità/Fate (1892)* and *Tempeste/Tempests (1895)*, catapults her career. These books unite the causes of proletarians and feminists in bitter, thorny, rebellious tones confined to themes of anxiety and discontent. They also represent the spiritual and material unease of the poet's own humble beginnings. Thus, she's proclaimed *la vergine rossa*, "the red virgin" of the new Socialism at home, and "the poet of democracy" abroad. She later publishes *Maternità/Motherhood* (1904), *Dal profondo/From the Deep* (1910), and *Esilio/Exile* (1914) — works that are more focused on personal experience.

In 1919, her second phase opens with the acclaimed *Il libro di Mara*, in essence one long poem arising from a woman's most intimate place as if in a visceral scream — a most passionate expression of love, loss and redemption. This phase shifts to divine contemplation in *I canti dell'isola*, yet sustains the driving impulse of *Il libro di Mara*.[5]

---

4. en.wikipedia.org
5. A new dual-language edition: *The Book of Mara*, translated by Maria A. Costantini (New York: Italica Press, 2011).

Even so, Negri's island songs of love are seemingly in discord with herself as she wanders dreamily across this new-found paradise of grace and blossomed branches. In *La sofferenza/Suffering*, the poet realizes that her pain is without cure: *Non credevi soffrire così, donna, ancora così*.... / You didn't believe you'd be suffering like this, woman, still like this....

Her third and final phase, consisting of *Vespertina (1930) Il dono/The Gift* (1936) and *Fons Amoris (1946)*, is her most introspective and spiritual, turning increasingly to religion.

Of Ada Negri's ten volumes of poetry, one was published posthumously.

Interest in Negri's work declined rapidly in the post-war period when her link to Mussolini and the Fascists was severely criticized. And, with a few exceptions, her work was abandoned in the late Fifties/early Sixties. In addition to the probable reason already mentioned, various critics said that her writing often had an undeniable propensity in tone both academic and mannerist. They contended that her second phase, considered the pinnacle of her artistic work, was indebted not only to strong influences by the "three crowns" of poetry: Carducci-Pascoli-D'Annunzio, but also by Walt Whitman.

Benedetto Croce, the most influential literary critic of the first half of the twentieth century, categorized Ada Negri's work as "facile, tearful, completely centered on the melodiousness and readiness of emotions — poetics that are somewhat melancholy, idyllic-elegiac."[6] He dismissed her work by stating that "lack or imperfection in artistic work is most particularly a feminine flaw *(difetto femminile)*. It is precisely woman's maternal instinct, her 'stupendous and all-consuming' ability to mother a child that prevents

---

6. Lucia Re, "Futurism and Fascism, 1914-1945," in *A History of Women's Writing in Italy,* edited by Letizia Panizza and Sharon Wood (Cambridge: Cambridge University Press 2000), pp.190–91.

her from successfully giving birth to a fully realized literary work."[7]

By contrast, critic, scholar and poet, Vincenzo Schilirò posed that to understand the poetry of an author, there is only one plausible way: to know the soul of the poet. He said that Negri's art indeed shines of a flame and an interior light: veiled and smoky at times, but always vibrant and powerful. Her poetry is the breath of her soul. We can view this poet/author, affectionately called *Dinin*, as "someone whose vision focused on the toils of life in a way few other writers did during those troubled times. Her naturally lyrical soul knew, in the major parts of her works, how to transform with an imprint of originality the sufferings, the bitterness, the joys of an entire generation."[8]

IV. Further Thoughts

Clearly, Negri's work doesn't draw a differentiating line between life and art. A poet of temperament, lyrical and profound, she escapes analysis. Writer/translator Ettore Romagnoli, as quoted in the newspaper *Liberal*, asserts that Negri "abolished established conventions, and shaped her lyrics according to the rhythms of the heart, in sync to whatever it is that makes the winds blow, gives rise to the waters and pulse to the stars — a poetry infinitely free, capricious and precise."[9]

In her article "Ada Negri between Earth and Sky," Teresa Madonna writes that "Negri's poetry cannot be judged according to designs and moralistic prescriptions, or according to a certain set of aesthetics, as Croce did, because the personal "I" of her poetry is the "I" that generates the universal."[10] Throughout *I canti*, we witness the serene

7. Idem.
8. Schilirò, pp. 23–26.
9. Filippo Maria Battaglia, "Una Calliope passionaria," *Liberal* (01/22/2009): 18. Web: www.liberal.it, Retrieved 06/2010.
10. Teresa Madonna, "Ada Negri tra terra e cielo," *Non T'ho Perduta* (Lodi: Associazione Poesia la Vita, 2006), p. 46.

transfiguration of Capri's dazzling landscape into the landscape of the soul. Madonna specifies that this poetry is set forth in a similar mould as Mara's lamentations in *Il libro di Mara*, only, here, the melodic element sweetens: "the lover, no longer weighted by flesh, appears in the fabled light of the moon above the magic waters of Capri."[11]

Yet, even while captive to Capri's mermaid cliffs "suspended in the ethereal essence of clouds," "necklaces of dreams," whispering cypresses and dog roses, the poet calls out to her daughter Bianca, to her grandchild Donata, and to the warm brown earth she can touch and is most vital to her being — the earth she wants to be buried in. She reclaims the love of her native Lombardy, the ancestral roots of her people. "The Village of My Mother" is a surge of filial pride, nostalgia for the Lombard mist, the steaming irrigation ditches, "square fields enclosed by mulberry trees," wherein sink the roots of those one can never deceive. The poem closes with a verse from a 1915 Lombard anti-war song, *Tamburino del reggimento/The Regiment's Tambourine: La Violetta la va...la va....* The long-traveled song of *Tamburino*, and the hero's medal no one remembers.

The poetic arc of *I canti* concludes with the expectation of death; a death that is serene and, at last, consoling. *Corale notturno/Night Chorus* preludes the poet's ultimate resting place:

Quando sarò sepolta nel paese di mia madre,
là dove la bruma confonde i fertili solchi
terrestri, coi solchi del cielo,
le rane ed i rospi dei fossi mi canteranno la nenia notturna.

When I am buried in the village of my mother,
there where the mist mingles the fertile
furrows of earth with the furrows of sky,
the frogs and toads in the ditches will sing
their nightly dirge to me.

---

11. Madonna, pp. 47–48

INTRODUCTION   XIX

One might ask, would the poet have missed it as much, loved it as much, had she not been away, had she not been reborn on that paradise island?

VII. Translator's Notes

As I approach the translation of Ada Negri's poetry, I keep in mind the period of time it was written in, the position of women writers in what was then a predominantly male context, the pressures and criticisms imposed on these women, the courage of their work, and the indomitability of their spirit.

In the winter of 2006, during a critical period in my life, I discovered Ada Negri as a result of a web search on Italian women poets. As a teacher of English Literature and of Italian as a foreign language, I was troubled by the fact that in Italian anthologies of the nineteenth and twentieth centuries, the only woman represented was Sappho, and nominally so.

Excitedly, I began to read Negri's poems and felt an immediate connection. On further research, I discovered that there were virtually no published English translations of her books of poetry, except for *Fate*, by A.M. von Blomberg, in 1904. I learned that a number of Negri's "art" poems were set to music by Ottorino Respighi, particularly ones from her early period. I also read that her poetry is largely considered untranslatable. Wanting to find out why, I took on the challenge. Shortly before that, the only translation work I had done was a Pascoli poem in terza rima, *Il transito/The Transit*—an experience I found both maddening and riveting.

The poetry of *I canti dell'isola*, while mesmerizing, abounds in archaic Italian diction and syntax, prepositions that don't transfer to English, punctuation and couplets that need restructuring for clarity in English. For example, in *Euforbia/Euphorbia*, *l'arsura del luglio ti veste d'un drappo vinoso, di baccante ebbra*, required countless revisions. Here's an earlier version: "The dry heat of July dresses you in the drape of a reveling drunk." And the more loyal, "the burning heat of July clothes you in a vinous drape, an inebriate bacchante." In the same poem, *per lui disvellerti al sasso che t'è parte viva non puoi—né esso può*, started out as, "you can't break free from the living stone that's partly your life, for him—nor can he," and became more clear as, "you can't break free from the living stone for him—nor can he."

The biggest challenge in *Filastrocca/Nursery Rhyme* was the metaphorical first line, *Sette fiammelle di barche, che vanno a pescare*, which seemed impossible to render. I finally decided on a simile: "Like little flames, seven boats out to fish in the sea."

In the end, presupposing the translator is well-versed in both languages, I believe it is important to remain as loyal as possible to the original work, thereby preserving the integrity and spark of its creative force, and to honor it by finding a way to re-create it nearly as brilliantly in the target language.

Maria A. Costantini

Note: All citations of Italian origin are my own translation.

Glossary/Annotations

See frontispiece map for locations.

Àstrico: for construction, it is made by mixing *pozzolana* (Roman concrete), inert materials and lime. This is then used as foundation for brick floors.

Blue Grotto: a noted sea cave on the coast of the island of **Capri**. The cave is entered by a semi-circular opening just large enough to admit a rowboat. Sunlight, passing through an underwater cavity and shining through the seawater, creates a blue reflection that illuminates the cavern.

Capri: an Italian island in the Tyrrhenian Sea off the Sorrentine Peninsula, on the south side of the Gulf of Naples, in the Campania region of Southern Italy. It has been a resort since the time of the Roman Republic.

Features of the island are its 65 grottoes, the Belvedere of Tragara, which is a high panoramic promenade lined with villas, the limestone masses called Sea Stacks that stand out of the sea (the *Faraglioni*), Anacapri, the **Blue Grotto** (*Grotta Azzurra*), and the ruins of the Imperial Roman villas.

The City of Capri is the main center of population on Capri. It has two harbors, Marina Piccola and Marina Grande (the main port of the island). The separate commune of Anacapri is located high on the hills to the west.

The etymology of the name Capri can be traced back to the Greeks, the first recorded colonists to populate the island. This means that "Capri" was probably not derived from the Latin "Capreae" (goats), but rather the Greek "Kapros" (wild boar).

Casa Dòmina: a poem dedicated to the memory of Luisa Vismara, the mother of the engineer Emerico Vismara (a friend of Negri's), who built Villa Vismara circa 1920 on

Tragara Point, overlooking the rock formations of the *Faraglioni*. Following instructions from famed architect Le Corbusier, Vismara built a residence that was to be born out of the rock itself and become a refuge in which to find solace for the body, heart and soul. Since there is no record of a Casa Dòmina in Tragara, it is possible that Negri was referring to Villa Vismara (now Hotel Villa Tragara).

Cressida: a character who appears in medieval and Renaissance retellings of the Trojan War. She is a Trojan woman, the daughter of Calchas, a priestly defector to the Greeks. She falls in love with Troilus, the youngest son of King Priam, and pledges everlasting love, but when she is sent to the Greeks as hostage, she forms a liaison with the Greek warrior, Diomedes. Negri's placement of a slave-girl named Cressida in the poem *Il Rosaio* adds to the mythical context of the poem. The master in the poem may or may not allude to the Greek warrior.

Euforbia/**Euphorbia:** Negri's poem probably refers to *Euphorbia tirucalli*, a poisonous plant that has unmistakable, brush-like branch masses, a noticeable feature of the plant. The plant oozes a milky sap when damaged or cut. Contact with this sap may cause dermatitis in some people, and in the eyes the sap can cause temporary blindness.

Green Grotto: this "undiscovered" cave features the same luminescent glow as the **Blue Grotto.**

Grotto of the Great Mother: *Mater Magna* is a cave that goes by several other names: *Magnum Mithrae Antrum,* Italianized to *Mitromania, Matromania,* or *Matermania,* sometimes popularly called *Grotta del Matrimonio* (wedding cave). It is near the Natural Arc and its name is believed to derive from the goddess Cybele, aka *Mater Magna.* It is the only grotto in Capri accessible by land.

Grotto of Wonders: also known as the Marvelous Grotto. Approached by sea, there is an external staircase cut into the rock wall, and together with the White Grotto, these grottoes offer astonishing, spectacular formations of stalactites in which the color of the sea gives remarkable reflections.

Il Castiglione: there are ruins of two medieval castles on Capri: *Castello di Barbarossa* and *Il Castiglione* built at the peak of Mount Castiglione, probably between the tenth and eleventh centuries. They were to provide the inhabitants of Capri a secure, high place to take refuge in case of danger

Mount Tiberius: a mountain that rises to 334 meters at the eastern end of the island. It was named for the Emperor Tiberius who, in 30 A.D, built his Villa Jovis at the mountain's peak.

Morena: a feminine name meaning a girl or woman with brown or black hair, often with dark eyes and a relatively dark or olive complexion, derived from the Italian word *moro*, Moor.

Mount Èchele: one of the three mountains on the Asiago Plateau where, in 1918, a major World War I battle took place. Among the Alpine soldiers killed was Roberto Sarfatti, the seventeen-year-old son of Negri's best friend, Margherita Sarfatti. There is a monument erected in his honor on the site of the battle. Negri refers to this young man in her poem *Canzone bretone*.

Mount Solaro: the highest part of Capri, towering 589 meters above sea level and boasting a 360° panorama of the island of Capri. Mount Solaro is also called "Acchiappanuvole" or "cloud catcher" because of the thick blanket of fog which forms around the summit, especially at dawn, when the thermal difference between the sea and the rock is accentuated. The warmer, damper sea air condenses in a dense mist on the ground, the temperature of which is notably diminished during the night. Where its path is obstructed, the vapors rise upwards, generating a characteristic crown of clouds. This phenomenon also occurs in the evening, especially in the autumn. The wind clears away some of the clouds, randomly revealing various segments of the beautiful island landscape below.

Point Carena: or *Punta Carena*, is situated on the far southwest of the island of Capri, on the Limmo peninsula, which derives its name from the latin *limen* meaning boundary. Behind Point Carena looms the precipice of the Migliera, lined with defense walls built by the British in the 1800s in order to protect Capri from invasion.

Sea of Ulysses: Negri is no doubt referring to the Tyrrhenian triangle from Naples to Capri to Sicily, which was part of Ulysses' journey. The siren sisters in Greek Mythology, Ligeia, Leucosia, and Parthenope—half-women, half-birdlike creatures — were daughters of Melpomene, the Muse of Tragedy, and the River God Achelous. According to legend they lived on an island in the Tyrrhenian Sea and with their haunting music they lured sailors passing by into their trap and ultimate death.

Solaria: (plural for *solarium*) a room used especially for sunbathing or therapeutic exposure to light. Negri addresses two poems to Solaria, indicating that the appellation is meant to mean the solar island of Capri.

Tragara: on Capri's southeast tip is Tragara Road, which leads to Tragara Point, where a panoramic terrace overlooks the gigantic *Faraglioni* and the Bay of Marina Piccola on the Tyrhennain Sea.

Valkyrie: in *Il sagrato/The Churchyard*, Negri addresses Capri as a Tyrrhenian Valkyrie, further personifying the powers of the island. In Norse mythology, a Valkyrie is one of a host of female figures who decide who will die in battle. They bring their chosen to the afterlife hall of the slain, Valhalla, ruled over by the god Odin.

BIBLIOGRAPHY

This bibliography is indebted to Patrizia Zambon of the Dipartimento di Italianistica Università degli Studi di Padova and her website at http://www.maldura.unipd.it/italianistica/ALI/negri.html

ADA NEGRI'S WORKS

POETRY
Fatalità. Milan: Treves, 1892.
Tempeste. Milan: Treves, 1896.
Maternità. Milan: Treves, 1904.
Dal profondo. Milan: Treves, 1910.
Esilio. Milan: Treves, 1914.
Il libro di Mara. Milan: Treves, 1919.
I canti dell'isola. Milan: Mondadori, 1925.
Vespertina. Milan: Mondadori, 1930.
Il dono. Milan: Mondadori, 1936.
Fons amoris. Milan: Mondadori, 1946.

PROSE STORIES
Le solitarie. Milan: Treves, 1917.
Orazioni. Milan: Treves, 1918.
Finestre alte. Milan: Mondadori, 1923.
Le strade. Milan: Mondadori, 1926.
Sorelle. Milan: Mondadori, 1929.
Di giorno in giorno. Milan: Mondadori, 1932.
Erba sul sagrato. Milan: Mondadori, 1939.
Oltre. Milan: Mondadori, 1947.

NOVEL
Stella mattutina. Milan: Mondadori, 1921.
—. Reprint ed. Milan: Mondadori, 1970.
—. Edited by Gianguido Scalfi e Anna Folli. Milan: La Vita Felice, 1995.
—. Edited by Maristella Lippolis e Maria Rosa Cutrufelli. Pescara: Tracce, 1995.

VARIOUS
Alessandrina Ravizza. Milan: Società Umanitaria Fondazione P. M. Loria,1915.
Traduzione di *Storia di Manon Lescaut e del Cavaliere di Grieux*, di Antoine François Prévost. Milan: Mondadori, 1931.
53 Art Poems of Ada Negri's were set to music by Ottorino Respighi and various other composers from 1911 through 1991. Catalogo del Polo BNCF. Biblioteca Centrale di Firenze.

LETTERS
"Nell'inverno del '42, tra i fuochi di guerra, una lettera a un'amica crocerossina." In *Avvenire* 11 January 1995.
Buzzi, Paolo. *Futurismo. Scritti, carteggi, testimonianze III*. Edited by Mario Morini and Giampaolo Pignatari. Milan: Biblioteca Comunale di Milano, 1983.
Comes, Salvatore. *Ada Negri. Da un tempo all'altro*. Milan: Mondadori, 1970.
Cremascoli, Luigi. *Lettere di Ada Negri nella Biblioteca Laudense*. In *Archivio storico lodigiano* 2.1 (1954).
—. *Lettere di Ada Negri in un carteggio privato*. In *Archivio storico lodigiano* 2.2 (1954).
Fraticelli, Vincenzo. *Incontri con Ada Negri*. Naples: Conti, 1954.
Gennaro, Salvatore. *Una piccola amicizia di Ada Negri*. Olgiate Olona (Varese): Grafica Olona, 1995.
Mondrone, Domenico. *Scrittori al traguardo*. Rome: La Civiltà cattolica, 1947.
Negri, Ada, and Paolo Buzzi. *Diorami lombardi. Carteggio (1896–1944)*. Edited by Barbara Stagnitti. Padova: Il Poligrafo, 2008.
Pea, Mauro. *Due anime. Testimonianze religiose e letterarie dal carteggio inedito Ada Negri — Federico Binaghi*. Lodi: Edizioni Besana Brianza, 1986.
Pignatari, Giampaolo. *"Carteggio Ada Negri — Paolo Buzzi."* In *La Martinella di Milano* 34 (1980): 9–10.
Repossi, Cesare. *Cesare Angelini e Ada Negri. Incontri nella "rossa Pavia."* Pavia: Unitre, 1996.

BIBLIOGRAPHY OF CURATED WORKS SINCE 1970
L'appuntamento. In *Novelle d'autrice tra Otto e Novecento.* Edited by Patrizia Zambon. Rome: Bulzoni, 1998.
La Cacciatora e altri racconti. Edited by Antonia Arslan and Anna Folli. Milan: Scheiwiller, 1988.
La Cacciatora. In *Maestrine. Dieci racconti e un ritratto.* Edited by Vincenzo Campo. Palermo: Sellerio, 2000.
Le cartoline della nonna. Florence: Giunti e Nardini, 1973.
Clarissa. In *Novelle d'autrice tra Ottocento e Novecento.* Edited by Patrizia Zambon. Padova: Nuova Vita, 1987.
Mia giovinezza. Edited by Davide Rondoni. Milan: Rizzoli 1995.
Opere scelte. Edited by Elena Cazzulani and Gilberto Coletto. Lodi: Edizioni del Campus, 1984; Lodi: Lodigraf, 1988.
Opere scelte. Edited by Elena Cazzulani and Angela Gorini Santoli. Lodi: Il Pomerio, 1995.
Poesie. Edited by Silvio Raffo. Milan: Mondadori, 2002.
Translation of Antoine François Prévost. *Manon Lescaut.* Milan: ES, 1992.

ANTHOLOGIZED WORKS
Scrittrici d'Italia. Edited by Alma Forlani e Marta Savini. Rome: Newton Compton, 1991.
L'altro sguardo. Antologia delle poetesse del '900. Edited by Guido Davico Bonino and Paola Mastrocola. Milan: Mondadori, 1996.
Capriccio e coscienza. Scrittrici fra due secoli. Edited by Marino Biondi and Simona Moretti. Cesena: Società Editrice "Il Ponte Vecchio," 1997.
Miserabili in poesia. Criminali, marginali e vittime in versi contemporanei. Edited by Giovanni Greco and Davide Monda. Rome: Carocci, 2002.

Secondary Works Since 1970

Aa. Vv. *Incontri con Ada Negri*. Lodi: Associazione "Poesia, la Vita," 1995.

Aa. Vv. *Ada Negri: "Parole e ritmo sgorgan per incanto."* Pisa-Rome: Giardini Editori e Stampatori in Pisa, 2007.

Abbrugiati, Perle. "Les visages de la solitude dans les nouvelles d'Ada Negri." In *Les femmes écrivains en Italie aux XIXe et XXe siècles*. Centre Aixois de Recherches Italiennes. Aix-en-Provence: Publications de l'Université de Provence, 1993.

Angelini, Cesare. *Cronachette di letteratura contemporanea. 1919–1971*. Bologna: Boni, 1971.

—. *Trenta lettere*. Edited by Angelo Stella and Angelo Comini. Pavia: Almo Collegio Borromeo, 1981.

—. *I doni della vita. Lettere 1913–1976*. Edited by Angelo Stella and Anna Modena. Milan: Rusconi, 1985.

Arslan, Antonia. *Dame, galline e regine. La scrittura femminile italiana fra '800 e '900*. Milan: Guerini e Associati, 1998.

Baggio, Cristina. "Il mondo interiore di Ada visto attraverso i suoi epistolari." In *Sulle orme*.

Bellio, Anna. "Ada Negri e 'Poesia'." *Rivista di Letteratura italiana* 24.2 (2006).

Comes, Salvatore. *Ada Negri. Da un tempo all'altro*. Milan: Mondadori, 1970.

Cossu Maria Grazia. *Lo specchio di Venere. La scrittura autobiografica di Neera, Ada Negri, Marina Jarre e Lalla Romano*. Sassari: Editrice Democratica Sarda, 2009.

De Troja, Elisabetta. "Le lettere di Ada ad Ettore Patrizi." In *Sulle orme*.

—. "Solitudine e solitudini in Ada Negri." In *Le forme del narrare*. Florence: Polistampa, 2004.

Dolfi, Anna et al. *Memorie, autobiografie e diari nella letteratura italiana dell'Ottocento e del Novecento*. Pisa: Edizioni ETS, 2008.

Farina, Domenico. "L'ultima Ada Negri." In *L'Osservatore politico letterario* 16.11 (1970).

Farnetti, Monica. *Il giuoco del maligno. Il racconto fantastico nella letteratura italiana tra Otto e Novecento*. Florence: Vallecchi, 1988.

Folli, Anna. "Lettura di Ada Negri." In *Svelamento. Sibilla Aleramo: Una biografia intellettuale*. Edited by Annarita Buttafuoco. Milan: Feltrinelli, 1988.

—. "Sono ammalata d'anima. Ada Negri tra 'Fatalità' e 'Tempeste'." In *Les femmes — écrivains en Italie (1870-1920): Ordres et libertés*. Edited by Emmanuelle Genevois. Paris: Chroniques Italiennes — Université de la Sorbonne Nouvelle, 1994.

—. *Penne leggère. Neera, Ada Negri, Sibilla Aleramo. Scritture femminili italiane fra Otto e Novecento*. Milan: Guerini e Associati, 2000.

Gambaro, Elisa. "Stella mattutina. L'autobiografia regressiva di Ada Negri." In Dolfi, *Memorie*.

Giardini, Laura. "Le lettere di Ada Negri conservate nei Fondi del Gabinetto G.P. Vieusseux di Firenze. Il rapporto con 'Il Marzocco' e gli Orvieto." In *Sulle orme*.

Gorini Santoli, Angela. *Invito alla lettura di Ada Negri*. Milan: Mursia, 1995.

Mattalia, Daniele. *Ada Negri. Dal dilettantismo sociale all'estetismo piccolo borghese*. In *Novecento*. Milan: Marzorati, 1979.

Mazzoni, Cristina. "Difference, Repetition, and the Mother–Daughter Bond in Ada Negri." *Rivista di Studi italiani* 15.1 (1997).

—. "Impressive Cravings, Impressionable Bodies: Pregnancy and Desire from Cesare Lombroso to Ada Negri." *Annali d'Italianistica* 15.15 (1997).

Merry, Bruce. "Ada Negri: Social Injustice and an Early Italian Feminist." *Forum for Modern Language Studies*, 26.3 (1988).

Palombi Cataldi, Anna Maria. *Solaria. La Capri magica di Ada Negri*. Naples: Grimaldi & Cicerano, 1984.

Paris, Renzo. *Il mito del proletariato nel romanzo italiano*. Milan: Garzanti, 1977.

Pastorino, Nadia. "Il carteggio Ada Negri — Umberto Fracchia." In *Sulle orme.*
Pea, Mauro. *Ada Negri.* Milan: Mondadori, 1970.
Petrocchi, Giorgio. "Per il centenario di Ada Negri." In *Nuova Antologia* 105.2037 (1970).
Pickering-Iazzi, Robin. "The Politics of Gender and Genre in Italian Women's Autobiography of the Interwar Years." *Italica* 71.2 (1994).
Rasy, Elisabetta. *Ritratti di signora.* Milan: Rizzoli, 1995.
Ruschioni, Ada. *Dalla Deledda a Pavese.* Milan: Vita e Pensiero, 1977.
—. *Poesia e metafisica della luce.* Milan: Vita e Pensiero, 1987.
Sebastiani, Roberta. "La fortuna di Ada Negri nella letteratura russa." *Archivio storico lodigiano* 31.12 (1993).
Spaziani, Maria Luisa. *Donne in poesia.* Venezia: Marsilio, 1992.
Sulle orme di Ada Negri. Lodi: Associazione "Poesia, la Vita," 2003.
Tortora, Matilde. "Un'autobiografia trasposta. Le lettere inedite di Ada Negri a Eleonora Duse." In Dolfi, *Memorie.*
Ulivi, Ferruccio. "Il centenario di Ada Negri." *Galleria* 21.6 (1971).
Vené, Gian Franco. *Gli operai superuomini di Ada Negri.* In *Novecento.* Milan: Marzorati, 1979.
Wood, Sharon. *Italian Women's Writing 1860–1994.* London: Athlone, 1995.
Zaccaro, Vanna. *Shaharazàd si racconta: Temi e figure nella letteratura femminile del Novecento.* Bari: Palomar, 2005.
Zambon, Patrizia. "Ada Negri, 'La Cacciatora e altri racconti'." *Studi novecenteschi* 17.39 (1990).
—. *Letteratura e stampa nel secondo Ottocento.* Alessandria: Edizioni dell'Orso, 1993.
—. "Ada Negri scrittrice." In *Sulle orme.*
Zimbone, Croce. *Luigi Capuana, Salvatore Farina, Arturo Graf, Ada Negri: Segnalazioni critiche.* Catania: Greco, 1981.

Songs of the Island

*Alle care Ombre
di Cesare e Roberto Sarfatti*

In memory of the beloved departed
Cesare and Roberto Sarfatti

Solaria

☀ Il male azzurro

Ho male di luce, ho male di te, Capri solare.
Oh, troppo bella, oh, simile all'onda sul capo
   del naufrago.
Ma forse ai miei occhi non sei che un raggiante
   capriccio del prisma,
una dorata nuvola emersa dal fiato del mare?
No. Sento il tuo cuore che vive, che batte,
   in un cavo di roccia
del Pizzolungo; e guardia dal mare gli fanno
   i Ciclopi
che mai non conobbero il sonno; e dal monte
   le lance
dell'àgavi, e immote, da torri di rupi,
   pupille di falchi.
Guizza ancor lungo i fianchi dei tre Ciclopi,
   e sfavilla
la lucertola azzurra che nacque al tuo nascere, o Capri.
Sacra al tempo, ella è maga, sovrana del
   sortilegio glauco.
Perfida come l'acqua che intorno agli scogli
   in cristalli
multispendenti s'indura, dissolti da un tuffo di remo,
s'io l'afferro mi sfugge e m'irride, lasciandomi
   agli occhi il barbaglio.
Azzurra è la tua follia, Capri, nube del mare.
Azzurro il canto eterno di che tu colmi i cieli.
S'io debba morire di te, dammi la morte azzurra.

Solaria

The Blue Curse

Light pains me; you pain me, luminous Capri.

Oh, too beautiful, oh, like the wave above the head
　of a castaway.

But perhaps, to my eyes, you are no more than the dazzling
　whim of a prism,

a gilded cloud emerged from the breath of the sea?

No. I feel your heart that lives, that beats,
　in a rock-cave

of Pizzolungo; and guarding it from the sea
　are the Cyclops,

who never knew sleep; and from the mountain
　the lances

of agave and, fixed, from the towering cliffs,
　the eyes of falcons.

Still darting alongside the three Cyclops,
　and sparkling,

is the blue she-lizard born at your birth, o Capri.

Sacred in time, she is a sorceress, queen
　of the blue-green spell.

Treacherous as the water that hardens around cliffs
　in glittering crystals,

dissolved at the plunge of an oar;

if I grasp her, she slips away and mocks me,
　leaving her glare in my eyes.

Blue is your folly, Capri, cloud of the sea.

Blue the eternal chant you use to fill your skies.

Should I die of you, grant me a blue death.

L'OFFERTA DELLE ROSE

Chi fu mai, che dall'alto del muro mi gettò
tre rose vermiglie?

Miravo, passando, il rosaio scalare il muro
come un amante

dai mille cuori per mille amori, cuori malati
di troppo sangue:

ed ecco, una mano dall'alto mi gettò tre rose
vermiglie:

per la fede, per la speranza, per la gioia che
ancora non so.

Fanciulli dell'Isola, in grazia, cercate per strade,
per boschi, per campi

colui che dall'alto del muro mi gettò tre rose
vermiglie:

conducetelo a me, ch'io lo veda, e gli dica
ch'egli è mio fratello:

e mangi con lui pane intriso di sole, e beva
acqua di libertà.

An Offer of Roses

Who was it that, from atop the wall, threw me
 three vermilion roses?

Passing by, I admired the rosebush climbing the wall
 like a lover

of a thousand hearts for a thousand loves — hearts aching
 from too much blood:

and there, a hand from up high threw me three
 vermilion roses:

for the faith, the hope, the joy I've yet
 to know.

Children of the Island, I pray you, search
 every street, every wood, every field,

for the one who, from atop the wall, threw me
 three vermilion roses:

lead him to me, that I may look upon him and tell him
 he's my brother:

and share with him bread dipped in the sun, and drink
 the water of freedom.

Notte di Capri

Così basse le stelle sul capo, che par mi
vogliano incoronare.

Se alzassi a pena – per gioco — la mano, forse
le potrei toccare.

Ma non ho forza d'alzar la mano: l'aria sa
troppo di rose bianche.

Rose e stelle si guardano, fisse, con occhi
immensi di donne stanche.

C'è così poco fra loro: un po' d'aria: solo
un po' d'aria; e non posson baciarsi.

C'e così poco fra me e te: un po' d'aria:
solo un po' d'aria: e non posso baciarti.

Tu sei nascosto; ma la tua vita chiama
nell'ombra i miei sensi veglianti.

Il mare è nascosto; ma il suo respiro empie
la notte di tutti i miei pianti.

Capri Night

So low are the stars above my head, it seems
   they want to crown me.

If I raised my hand a bit–playfully–maybe
   I could touch them.

But I lack the strength to raise my hand: the air
   tastes too much of white roses.

Roses and stars gaze at each other, intent,
   with the immense eyes of tired women.

There's so little between them: a little air: only
   a little air; and they cannot kiss each other.

There's so little between you and me: a little air:
   only a little air; and I cannot kiss you.

You are hidden; but into the shadow
   your life calls my waking senses.

The sea is hidden; but its breath fills
   the night with all my tears.

IL PERGOLATO DI GLICINI

Solaria, il vento del sud scrolla e devasta
  il tuo pergolato di glicini.

Ne piombano a terra i corimbi, chicchi
  violetti di grandine, pesanti d'un peso di morte.

Così a te traboccan dagli occhi, nell'ora
  del torbido amore, le lacrime;

ma non si raccoglie il pianto d'amore,
  non si raccolgono i fiori caduti del glicine.

The Wisteria Trellis

Solaria, the south wind shakes and destroys
   your trellis of wisteria.

Corymbs plunge to the ground like violet
   beads of hail, heavy as death.

Just like the tears that spill from your eyes
   in the turbid moment of love;

but no one gathers tears of love, no one
   gathers fallen wisteria blooms.

La cintura di giada

*Il mare, tuo re, magnifico amante, ti donò
una cintura di giada*

*che cinse egli stesso a' tuoi fianchi, Solaria,
regina dell'isole.*

*Nella sua gemmea sostanza, secondo
i capricci del sole,*

*s'incastonan le perle del pianto, e i diaspri
della passione,*

*e gli smeraldi della speranza, e le ametiste
della nostalgia.*

*E t'imprigiona e ti solca e a volte ti riga le
reni di sangue;*

*ma tu non puoi gettarla: la chiude, geloso,
il suggello del tuo signore.*

*Non v'ha forza al mondo — ne soffri e ne godi
— che spezzi il suggello d'amore.*

The Belt of Jade

The sea, your king, magnificent lover,
   gave you a belt of jade

that he himself tied around your hips, Solaria,
   queen of the islands.

In its gem-like substance, depending
   on the whims of the sun,

are embedded pearls of tears, and the jaspers
   of passion,

and the emeralds of hope, and the amethysts
   of nostalgia.

And it imprisons you and digs into you, at times
   leaving bloody grooves in your loins;

but you cannot cast it away: it is locked, jealously,
   by the seal of your lord.

There's no force in the world — this pleases
   and pains you — that could break the seal of love.

STANCHEZZA

*Or cercherai riposo, sotto i carrubi: ché gli
occhi*

*t'ha resi folli il sole dell'Isola folle. Ora gli
occhi*

*tu chiuderai, sull'erba: fin che l'abbaglio sia
spento.*

*Non sapevi che la bellezza fosse sì gran
patimento.*

*Agli aromi che intridon la macchia, per
dormire, chiederai grazia:*

*questa è terra senza pietà, di troppa delizia
ti macera e strazia.*

*Voci che amavi, che t'eran sì dolci, sì
necessarie, laggiù*

*al paese: voci del sangue: non son più tue,
non ti chiaman più.*

*Questa è terra senza pietà, ti ruba a te stessa,
ti svuota della memoria,*

*poi, con una risata di sole, ti scaglia a mare,
consunta scoria.*

*Se vuoi salvarti, vattene. — Domani sarà
troppo tardi.*

*Ma forse non vuoi salvarti. — Taci, allora.
Abbandónati. Ardi.*

Fatigue

Now you will look for rest, under the carob-trees:
since your eyes

are crazed from the sun of the mad Island. Now
you will close

your eyes, on the grass: until the bedazzlement
fades.

You didn't know that beauty could bring such
suffering.

To the aromas infusing the brush land,
you will ask for grace, so you may sleep.

This is a land without pity: it steeps you in too much
delight and torments you.

Voices you loved, once so sweet to you, so needed,
down there

in the village: voices of kinship: no longer yours,
they no longer call you.

This is a land without pity; it robs you of self,
it empties out memory,

then, with a laugh from the sun, it hurls you to sea,
used-up slag.

If you want to save yourself, leave. Tomorrow
will be too late.

But, maybe, you don't want to save yourself. Quiet, then.
Give in. Burn.

Sangue

*Fra l'erbe dàn sangue i papaveri: raccoglierli
   tutti non posso,*

*e quelli che colgo, morendo, mi si raggruman
   sul cuore.*

*Ma cento ne strappo e cento ne sgorgano, e
   l'Isola intera zampilla di rosso:*

chi l'ha ferita di coltello, chi l'ha ferita
   d'amore?

Blood

Among grasses, the poppies shed blood:
  I cannot pick them all,

and the ones I gather clot over my heart
  as they die.

But I tear off a hundred and one hundred emerge
  and the entire Island spurts out red:

who stabbed it with a knife, who stabbed it
  with love?

La nave

*Se il libeccio trascina le nubi per I capelli, e
ti squassa*

*da Monte Tiberio a Punta Carena, e dai due
golfi ti minaccia il mare:*

*o se l'azzurro ti circonfonde, e non sai qual
sia il mare o sia il cielo,*

*Isola della mia gioia, io palpito in te come
sul ponte d'una vasta nave.*

*Va con ciminiere fiorite di rose, con gomene
e sartie di verdi liane,*

*va col mio cuore d'evasa pulsante fra l'onde
e le stelle su prora di sogni,*

*nave corsara della bellezza, pel viaggio donde
io non ritorni più!*

The Ship

If the southwest wind drags the clouds by the hair,
   and jolts you

from Mount Tiberius to Point Carena, and the sea
   threatens you from its two gulfs;

or if the blue is all around you, and you don't know
   which is the sea and which is the sky,

Island of my joy, in you I throb as if on the deck
   of an immense ship.

Go with smokestacks blooming with roses, with hawsers
   and stays of green lianas,

go with my runaway heart beating between the waves
   and the stars on a bow of dreams,

corsair-ship of beauty, on a voyage from where
   I may never return!

✺ VERTIGINE

Per la strada rupestre scendevo, verso la
spiaggia delle Sirene,

e vidi che i rovi e i pinastri camminavano
con me.

Taciti volti, scavati dal tempo, protesi nel
vuoto incolmabile,

vidi che i picchi dei monti camminavano
con me.

Anche il cielo d'un torrido azzurro, anche i
massi degradanti al mare

si misero a camminare, e tutto camminò con
me.

Nel mondo fu, solo, quel cerchio, roteante
su aperte voragini

d'aria e d'acqua; ed in esso, perduto, il mio
piccolo cuore con me.

Sentii che cadevo, giù giù negli spazi; e forse
gridai, ma di gioia:

perché nel fondo tu eri, nel fondo mi avresti
ripresa, Signore, con te.

VERTIGO

Going down the rocky road, toward
  the beach of the Sirens,

I saw that the briers and cluster-pines
  walked with me.

Silent faces, dug out by time, outstretched
  in the unfillable void,

I saw that the mountaintops walked
  with me.

The sky too, of a torrid blue, and the boulders
  leaning to the sea

began to walk, and everything walked
  with me.

In the world, there was only that circle, whirling
  above open chasms

of air and of water; and in it, lost with me,
  my young heart.

I felt myself falling, down, down into spaces;
  and maybe I screamed, but from joy:

because you were at the bottom, and
  at the bottom you would have taken me,

Lord, back with you.

La luna scende in giardino

La luna scende in giardino per le scale
della pallida sera:

è tutta bella, le nubi la velano, la brezza la
scopre.

S'attarda dietro il cipresso, s'aggrappa
all'agavi e ai fichi d'India,

stende trine leggere sui viali, lega le fronde
con fili d'argento,

nell'ombra screziata di raggi crea e dissolve
danze di gnomi,

con le perle della rugiada sfila e infila
collane di sogni.

So che sul mare è nata una strada, una bianca
strada

per chi vuole arrivare la notte alle reggie
di Dio.

Vada chi vuole sulla bianca strada, vada chi
vuole con barca e con vela:

a me piace restare in giardino a giocar con i
raggi e con l'ombre.

Due stelle — sole — accanto alla luna: due
larghe pupille serene.

Dove sei tu, che mi amavi, e mi dicevi:
"Dinin, mio bene"?

The Moon Descends on the Garden

The moon descends on the garden down the steps
  of the pale evening:

it's full of beauty, veiled by the clouds, bared
  by the breeze.

It lingers behind the cypress, clings
  to the agave and prickly pears,

spreads lacework over paths, binds the foliage
  with silver threads,

in shadows speckled with moonbeams, it creates
  and dissolves dances of gnomes,

with pearls of dew it threads and unthreads
  necklaces of dreams.

I know that a road is born on the sea, a white
  road

for those who wish to reach God's palace
  in the night.

Let them take the white road, if they wish; let them
  take a sailboat, if they wish:

I like to stay in the garden to play
  with the rays and the shadows.

Two stars—alone—next to the moon: two
  wide tranquil eyes.

Where are you, who loved me, and used to say:
  Dinin, my beloved?

COROLLE

☀ RIFUGIO FIORITO

Contro la porta chiusa, grovigli di rose canine:

dentro, tre palmi di terra, e un cactus con
grappe violette armate di spine.

C'è, anche, un geranio. Sgorgò da uno
spacco, per uno scherzo dei vènti.

Oggi è il padrone: crepita, in tutti i suoi
tizzi ardenti.

Vorrebbe il cactus bruciare a quel rogo:
striscia e s'abbarbica, con ansia muta,

mordendo la terra. C'e un muro di rose
contro la porta. La chiave è perduta.

Se quella porta s'aprisse, con la tua ombra
là dentro sostare

vorrei; né più udir voce d'uomini, voce di
mare.

Striscerei verso te, contro te, come verso il
geranio di bragia del cactus le spire:

barricherei la porta col mio amore cangiato
in rosaio, per non lasciarti partire.

Dalla tua ombra saprei, finalmente, se è vero
che hai detto il mio nome

in punto di morte: non puoi non aver detto
il mio nome.

Corollas

❋   Refuge in Bloom

Against the closed door, snarls of dog roses:

inside, three spans of dirt, and a cactus
  with clusters of violets armed with thorns.

There's also a geranium. It sprang through
  a crack, by a jest of the winds.

Today it is master: it crackles, in all its
  flaming embers.

It seems the cactus wants to burn on that pyre:
  it creeps and clings, with quiet longing,

biting the dirt. There's a wall of roses
  against the door. The key is lost.

If that door were to open, I would want to pause
  with your shadow

inside; no longer hear the voice of men,
  the voice of the sea.

I would crawl toward you, against you, like the spines
  of the cactus toward the geranium's embers:

with my love changed into a rosebush,
  I would barricade the door, not to let you go.

From your shadow I would know, at last, if it is true
  that you said my name

the moment you died: you can't not have said
  my name.

Per la tomba

Rose di porpora, ne ho piene le braccia,
sulla tua tomba le vorrei portare:

ma la tua tomba è di là dal monte, le tua
tomba è di là dal mare.

Rose di porpora, le lascerò, grandi e stanche,
sfogliarsi al mio piede:

poiché tomba verace io ti sono, io ti accolgo
e ti confesso in fede.

For the Tomb

Purple roses, my arms are filled with them,
   I would bring them to your tomb:

but your tomb is on the other side of the mountain,
   your tomb is on the other side of the sea.

Purple roses, I will let them, large and tired,
   shed their petals at my feet:

since I am your true tomb, I receive you
   and confess you in faith.

Fiori, soavi fiori

*Passo passo m'accompagnate lungo i giardini
dell'Isola,*

fiori, soavi fiori,

*e tanti siete, e diversi, e sì belli ch'è vano
chiamarvi per nome,*

fiori, soavi fiori,

*ed io non oso toccarvi, tremando di offendervi
pur col mio fiato.*

*Eppure, voi, labbra dischiuse, voi, carne
vivente e splendente,*

*parole mi dite, delizie mi date che sin
nell'occulto mi turbano*

*ove solo potè col suo amore l'uomo che solo
ho amato:*

fiori, soavi fiori,

*quando fra quelle braccia morire mi parve
e la vita fu.*

Flowers, Gentle Flowers

Step by step, you accompany me along
   the gardens of the Island,

flowers, gentle flowers,

you are many, diverse, and of such beauty
   that it's futile to call you by name,

flowers, gentle flowers,

and I do not dare touch you, afraid I might hurt
   you even with my breath.

And yet, you, lips semi-open, you, living
   resplendent flesh,

tell me words, give me delights that perturb
   me to the core

where only the only man I loved could reach me
   with his love:

flowers, gentle flowers,

when it seemed I had died in those arms —
   and life came to be.

Ada Negri

Euforbia

*Nutrita di roccia, tu affondi nella roccia le
  tue radici*

*e t'è impresso sul volto di fiore il mistero
  della madre pietra.*

*Splendi in aprile come un disco d'oro,
  trascolori sulfurea nel maggio:*

*l'arsura del luglio ti veste d'un drappo vinoso,
  di baccante ebbra.*

*Innamorata del fico d'India dalle innumeri
  mani in preghiera,*

*per lui disvellerti al sasso che t'è parte viva
  non puoi — né esso può;*

*e ti dilati, impura, gonfia di tossico, nel
  desiderio vano.*

*O velenosa, sei bella; ma niun s'attenta a
  toccare i tuoi fiori perfetti.*

*O solitaria, io conosco fra gli uomini un
  deserto ch'è simile al tuo.*

*O alta sul mare, un cuore io conosco ch'è
  più in alto e più triste di te.*

EUPHORBIA

Nourished by rock, in the rock you sink
  your roots

and imprinted in your flower's face is the mystery
  of the mother-stone.

In April you shine like a golden disc; in May
  your color pales to sulfur:

the burning heat of July clothes you in a vinous
  drape, an inebriate bacchante.

Enamored of the prickly pear with the countless
  hands in prayer,

you can't break free from the living stone
  for him — nor can he;

and you expand, impure, swollen with venom
  in that vain desire.

O poisonous one, you are beautiful; but no one
  dares touch your perfect flowers.

O solitary one, I know a desert among men
  resembling yours.

O high one above the sea, I know a heart
  that is up higher and sadder than you.

ADA NEGRI

VIOLA E NERO

Ho un tulipano viola, d'un viola intenso,
chiazzato di nero.

È il tuo gemello, bambina che vidi quest'oggi
ruzzar sul sentiero,

piccola, smorta, in tunica viola, d'un viola
intenso,

con la zazzera nera scomposta sui neri occhi
dallo sguardo immenso.

Violet and Black

I have a violet tulip, an intense violet,
 spotted in black.

It is your twin, young girl I saw today
 romping along the trail,

small, pale, in a violet tunic, an intense
 violet,

with a disheveled mass of black hair over black
 eyes with an immense gaze.

✺ LE TRE CORONE

Quando l'estate fende le pietre su gl'irti
 fianchi del Castiglione,

la sua vetta ha tre corone, tre corone di
 ginestre.

L'una è d'orgoglio, l'altra di gloria, terza è
 quella della passione:

le accende il sole, le difende il mare, cantano
 in esse i vènti:

e non t'importa il dolore delle piaghe nei
 fianchi roventi,

o Castiglione, se hai tre corone, tre corone
 di ginestre.

THE THREE CROWNS

When summer cleaves the stones on the rugged
  sides of Castiglione,

its summit has three crowns, three crowns
  of broom.

One is of pride, another is of glory, third
  is that of the passion:

the sun lights them, the sea defends them, the winds
  sing among them:

and you don't mind the painful sores
  on your scorching sides,

o Castiglione, as long as you have three crowns,
  three crowns of broom.

BENEDIZIONE

*Dolce nella memoria, mattino di festa, che
  in Capri io trovai*

*fiorita la chiesa di fresche fanciulle!
  Cantavano: "Stella maris,*

*rosa mystica, virgo pia"; e ciascuna teneva
  una rosa*

*in mano: alta e dritta sul vivido stelo, qual
  cero splendente.*

*Taciuto il coro, ogni rosa benedisse il
  ministro di Dio*

*con le stille del sacro aspersorio; e in ogni
  rosa la fede*

*che la porgeva; e l'arbusto donde amor la
  recise; e la zolla*

*che il primo seme ne accolse; e la casa serena
  che accanto*

*le sorge; e i padri, e i figli, ed i figli dei figli
  nel tempo.*

*Non rosa avevo io da offrire; ma il mio
  cuore, o Signore. Sbocciò*

*d'un tratto; e da quel giorno il mio cuore
  ha profumo di rosa.*

BENEDICTION

Sweet in my memory, a feast-day morning
  in Capri, when I found

the church in bloom with young girls!
  They were singing: "*Stella maris,*

rosa mystica, virgo pia;" and each one held
  a rose

in her hand: tall and straight on the vivid stem,
  like a shining candle.

The choir silent, God's minister blessed
  every rose

with drops of water from the sacred vessel;
  and in each rose he blessed

its offering of faith; the branch it was cut from
  with love: the earth

that received its first seed; the quiet house
  standing beside it;

the fathers, the children, and the children's children
  over time.

I had no rose to offer but my heart,
  o Lord. Of a sudden,

it blossomed; and since that day my heart
  has had the scent of a rose.

ADA NEGRI

L'uomo e la casa

☀ L'uomo e la casa

Uomo dell'Isola, tu la tua casa hai costrutta
con spasimo vivo di roccia

sulla montagna che guarda il mare d'Ulisse:
candida e nuda

tu l'hai costrutta, con archi lunati pieni di
cielo.

A picco sul mare d'Ulisse spalancate tu hai
le sue logge

per meglio affondar nell'immenso i tuoi occhi
di gemma turchina,

uguali ai duri smalti che finge il Tirreno
intorno agli scogli.

Il tetto antico d'àstrico imposto a l'eccelsa
tua casa tu hai;

e dodici uomini, a batterlo, secondo il
costume, chiamasti;

e vennero i dodici uomini, per rito, con
ferree mazzòccole.

Sotto la furia del sole calcaron, tre giorni,
nel grigio cemento l'ardente lapillo,

"Morena, mia Morena, aaaah, ooooh!"

scandendo sul battere alterno il canto ebbro,

The Man and the House

The Man and the House

Man of the Island, you built your house
  to the living pulse of the rock

on the mountain overlooking the sea of Ulysses:
  you built it

white and bare, with crescent arches
  full of sky.

A sheer drop to the sea of Ulysses, you've opened
  its balconies wide,

to better sink in its immensity your gemlike,
  turquoise eyes,

like the hard enamels the Tyrrhenian feigns
  around its reefs.

You laid the ancient roof of *àstrico* on your lofty
  house;

and, according to custom, you called upon
  twelve men to tap it down;

and the twelve men came, for the ritual,
  with iron mallets.

In the sun's furious heat they pounded, for three days,
  the burning lapillus into the gray cement,

"Morena, my Morena, aaaah, ooooh!"

alternating the strains of their euphoric song

signore dei cieli:

"Morena, io per te moro, aaaah, ooooh!"

✺

*Consacrata così la tua casa al nume solare
   e marino,*

*in essa, a colloquio con tre solitudini, l'acqua,
   la terra e il vento,*

*tu vivi, uomo dell'Isola, che il mondo hai
   percorso, ma qui le radici*

*affondi; e non ami nessuno, ma sol la tua
   terra tu ami, sol d'essa godi,*

*né pensi alla morte: ché uscito tu sei dalla
   stessa matrice di roccia*

*di che la tua casa hai costrutta; e, salso ed
   amaro, nelle vene ti scorre il Tirreno.*

with their pounding, lord of the skies:

"*Morena, I die for you, aaaah, ooooh!*"

Your house thus consecrated to the deity of the sun
   and the sea,

in it, in harmony with the three solitudes, water,
   earth, and wind,

you live, man of the Island, who traveled the world,
   yet here is where

you sink your roots; and you love no one,
   you love only your land, enjoying only her,

nor do you think of death: since you came from the
   same matrix of rock

you built your house with; and, salty and bitter,
   the Tyrrhenian flows in your veins.

La Casa Solitaria

"Sicut lilium inter spinas"

Viandante, se vai fino a Punta Tragara
argentea d'ulivi,

prendi, a sinistra, un viottolo scavato
a scaglioni nel sasso.

Aspro; ma verso il mare tutto oro di folli
ranuncoli,

verso il monte tutto ombre di mirti
e pensoso amaranto di cardi.

Ti condurrà alla casa che risponde, marmoreo
silenzio, ai silenzi dell'aria:

a quel cancello un giorno tremando io bussai,
mendica d'eternità.

Non si dischiuse il cancello, ch'è armato di
lance di ferro spinose

convergenti ad un cerchio ov'è infisso,
prigioniero del sogno, il mio cuore.

Non liberarlo: esso è il giglio vermiglio, che
scelse il suo cerchio di spine,

e là, soltanto, è felice: i monti dall'alto, dal
basso i marosi

gli favoleggian dell'alba in cui l'Isola apparve,
virginea, su l'onde;

e il vento gli porta, con murmuri densi di
bosco, lo strido dell'aquila.

Casa Solitaria
"As the lily among thorns"

Passerby, if you go as far as Tragara Point,
   silvery with olive trees,

take, on your left, a path hewn
   out of stone.

It is rough; but toward the sea it's all golden
   with wild buttercups,

toward the mountain it's all shaded with myrtle
   and pensive amaranth of thistles.

It will lead you to a house that answers, in marble
   silence, to the silences of the air:

one day I knocked on its gate, trembling,
   a beggar for eternity.

The gate would not open. It is armed
   with spiny lances of iron

that converge in a circle: there, my heart,
   prisoner of dreams, is inflicted.

Do not set it free: it is the vermillion lily
   that chose its circle of thorns,

and it is happy only there: the mountains on high,
   the breakers below,

tell it stories of the dawn when the island appeared,
   virginal, on waves;

and the wind, with dense forest murmurs,
   brings it the shriek of the eagle.

Il Rosaio

Nell'alta Anacapri, sorrisa da lucenti vitiferi
colli,

scopersi, fra boschi d'ulivi, una casa ch'è
detta Il Rosaio.

Qual le dia nome, ignoro: tanti intorno le
sboccian roseti

candidi e gialli; ma forse è il purpureo, che
il muro a levante

inghirlanda; e pur nell'inverno ha potenza
di fronde e di fiori.

Casa nomata Il Rosaio, oh, bene io vorrei
fra i tuoi orci d'argilla,

freschi al tatto nel portico basso, raccogliermi
in giorni di pace.

Ma non m'è dato. Restare non può nella
casa nomata Il Rosaio

se non Criseida la schiava, di quindici anni:
che intreccia

sulla soglia gli ondosi capelli, nell'ozio,
spiando con occhi di smalto

se dalla spiaggia o dal colle, duro al comando,
dolce all'amplesso, torni il padrone.

ROSAIO

In high Anacapri, graced by luminous
    vine-covered hills,

I discovered, among the olive groves, a house
    called *Rosaio*.

Which rosebush names it, I don't know: so many
    rose gardens, white and yellow,

bloom around it; but maybe it's the purple one
    wreathing the eastern

wall; and even in winter it bears
    foliage and flowers.

House named *Rosaio*, oh, how I'd love
    to gather my thoughts on tranquil days,

among your clay vases, cool to the touch,
    on the terrace below.

But I'm not allowed. No one can stay
    in the house named *Rosaio*,

but fifteen-year-old Cressida, the slave,
    who, on the doorstep,

braids her wavy hair in idleness,
    spying with her enamel eyes

whether, from the beach or the hill, the master,
    harsh of command, sweet in embrace, returns.

Canzoni dell'alba

☼ Mattutino

Voce che mi chiami, che mi dici: "Svégliati:"

*voce di bocca invisibile, di casto invisibile
   amore:*

*voce che sorgi dal sogno, ma sei della terra,
   e più dolce*

*mai non udii: son pronta: ti seguo: spalanco
   il balcone.*

*E l'alba color d'ametista mi arride dal tremulo
   mare,*

*con cenni di nuvole rosee mi riconosce dal
   cielo,*

*con fresco silenzio di fronde a me sospira
   dagli orti.*

*Nasce l'Isola bella con me dall'innocenza
   dell'acque,*

*nasce l'amore con me per le divine
   beatitudini,*

*nel nome del Padre, del Figlio e dello Spirito
   Santo.*

Songs of Dawn

☀ Matins

Voice that calls me, that tells me: *Awaken*:

voice of an invisible mouth, of chaste
   invisible love:

voice that rises from a dream, yet is of this earth,
   and I have never heard

one sweeter. I'm ready to follow you: I fling
   open the balcony doors.

And dawn, the color of amethyst, smiles on me
   from the tremulous sea,

with hints of roseate clouds it recognizes me
   from the sky,

with the cool silence of foliage it sighs to me
   from the gardens.

The beautiful Island is born with me from the waters'
   innocence,

love is born with me by the divine
   beatitudes,

in the name of the Father, of the Son,
   and of the Holy Spirit.

COLLOQUIO

Chiesi all'alba: "Per quale prodigio ti sei
svegliata così serena?"

"Sorella," rispose "stanotte dormivo
accanto alla luna piena."

"Per quale celeste comando, così fresca,
riprendi la strada?"

"Sorella," rispose "stanotte io mi tuffavo
nella rugiada."

"Chi tesse, nell'ombra dei cieli, i tuoi veli
di pallido argento?"

"Una stellina ignota, la più piccola del
firmamento."

Così errammo pel monte, cantando, empiendo
di fiori le mani:

a un tratto ella sparve, nel sole, per tornare,
più bella, domani.

Conversation

I asked the dawn: "By what miracle did you
   awaken so serene?"

"Sister," she answered, "last night I slept
   beside the full moon."

"By which rule of the heavens do you, so fresh,
   take up the road again?"

"Sister," she answered, "last night I dove
   into the dew."

"Who, in heaven's shadow, weaves your veils
   of pale silver?"

"An unknown little star, the smallest
   in the firmament."

Thus, we roamed about the mountain,
   singing, filling our hands with flowers:

of a sudden she vanished, in the sun, to return,
   more beautiful, tomorrow.

Addio della luna

La luna stilla un suo pianto d'oro nel mar
 di viola:

tacite lagrime d'alba, tristezza di
 partir sola.

Ad una ad una le stelle sono scomparse
 lontano:

tristezza d'aver camminato tutta la notte
 invano.

Si piega, sempre più stanca: affonda, sempre
 più smorta:

tristezza, innanzi alla vita, sparire senz'esser
 morta:

Pur le conviene obbedire al Sommo che la
 governa:

nel vuoto che non perdona, tristezza d'essere
 eterna.

The Moon's Goodbye

The moon sheds her golden tears into the
　violet sea:

they're silent tears of daybreak, the sadness
　of departing alone.

One by one, the stars have disappeared
　in the distance:

the sadness of having traveled all night
　in vain.

The moon folds in, more and more tired, sinks,
　more and more pale:

the sadness, before life, of vanishing
　without dying.

Yet, it's best she obey the Highest who
　rules her:

in the unforgiving void, the sadness of being
　eternal.

Ancora un giorno

*Sommesso gorgheggio d'uccelli, nell'ombra
più pallida.*

*Ancora un giorno, o mia vita, ancora un
giorno.*

Aprirsi di pupille arboree, brividire attonito.

*Per la tua speranza, per la tua salvezza,
ancora un giorno.*

*Forse oggi udrai la parola che già disperasti
di udire,*

*compirai l'atto che più non credevi da te
esser compiuto:*

*vittoria avrà il segno nel quale combatti,
avrà fine il patire:*

se tu cammini col tempo, nulla è perduto.

*Fra poco il pallore dell'ombra sarà gioia
ardente*

*di raggi, e saette di voli, del sole al
ritorno.*

*Riprendi te stessa, o mia vita, e sii tutta
presente:*

*per il tuo passaggio, per il tuo coraggio,
ancora un giorno.*

☀ ONE MORE DAY

A low warble of birds in the palest
  of shadows.

One more day, o my life, one more
  day.

Arboreal eyes open, an astounded shiver.

For your hope, for your salvation, one more
  day.

Maybe, today you will hear the words you've been
  despairing to hear;

you will accomplish the deed you no longer believed
  you'd accomplish:

your struggle will bear the mark of victory,
  your suffering will end:

if you walk with time, nothing is lost.

Soon the pallor of darkness will become
  an ardent joy

of light-beams, arrows in flight, from the returning
  sun.

Reclaim yourself, o my life, and be fully
  present:

for your passage, for your courage,
  one more day.

ADA NEGRI

La rugiada

*Tu che ti levi affranta dal tuo letto senza
  riposo*

e lasci dietro di te la tua notte senza speranza,

giungi le palme a coppa, tuffale nella rugiada,

fanne lavacro agli occhi, lavacro all'anima.

*Freschezza della rugiada, refrigerio più dolce
  del bacio*

*materno: ogni convolvolo è coppa di rosea
  rugiada,*

*il mare immenso è coppa di rosea rugiada,
  senz'orlo.*

Monte Solaro s'apre come un ventaglio roseo,

*sospesa ogni forma è nell'aria come nel sonno
  sognata,*

*l'aria è felice — e non sa del tuo pianto
  notturno.*

*Oh, smemorata e fluente alla luce, tu pure,
  tu pure!*

Verrà, fra poche ore verrà

*l'ombra che chiude i convolvoli, e te ricaccia
  sul letto di rovi*

*con la bocca contro il guanciale perché tu
  sola ti senta piangere.*

The Dew

You, who rise exhausted from your bed without
   rest

and leave behind your night without hope,

cup your hands together, dip them in dew,

make a wash for your eyes, a wash for your soul.

The freshness of dew, a comfort sweeter
   than the kiss

of a mother: every morning glory a cup of
   rose-colored dew,

the immense sea a cup of rose-colored dew,
   with no rim.

Mount Solaro opens like a rose-colored fan,

every shape suspended in air as if dreamed
   in a dream,

the air is glad — and doesn't know of your weeping
   at night.

Oh, you forget and flow to the light, you too,
   you too!

It will come, in a few hours the darkness
   that closes

the bindweed will come, and throw
   you back upon the bramble-bed,

mouth against the pillow so that you
   alone hear your weeping.

Ada Negri

La grande stella

M'apparve stanotte una stella sì viva, sì
    grande

che specchiava il suo volto nel mare, come
    la luna.

Forse era il volto materno, il segno della
    fortuna.

Mai sorrise più fulgido fiore fra le sideree
    ghirlande.

Capri, so che tu attiri le stelle nel grembo
    fragrante

de' tuoi mirteti; e, fra i baci, fino all'aurora
    le celi.

Vo cercando (ch'è presto l'aurora) quella che
    vidi sì sfolgorante;

ma invano. È fuggita la stella: è scomparsa
    nei cieli.

Presa e ben stretta l'avessi, stanotte, nella
    mia mano!

Levata come una lampada, andando andando
    senza sostare!

Forse condotta m'avrebbe — di là dalla terra
    e dal mare —

fino a lui, che sta troppo in alto, troppo
    lontano.

The Great Star

Tonight a star appeared to me so vibrant,
  so great

it reflected its face in the sea, like
  the moon.

Perhaps it was the face of a mother, the sign
  of good fortune.

There never was a more dazzling flower smiling
  in a garland of stars.

Capri, I know you lure the stars to the fragrant
  womb

of your myrtle groves; and you hide them 'til dawn
  in our kisses.

I am searching (for dawn is near) for that star
  so radiant;

but it's no use. The star has fled: disappeared
  in the skies.

Tonight, I would have caught it and held it tight
  in my hand!

I would have raised it like a lamp, going going
  without stopping!

Maybe it would have led me beyond the earth
  and the sea

all the way to him, who's too high up, too
  far away.

Ada Negri

Miraggi

Il segreto

Baciai la coccola del cipresso, nell'ombra
del cipresseto:

gioiosa, la coccola fulva mi donò, per il
bacio, un segreto.

Or che chiudo il segreto degli alberi nella
bocca dolceamara

più non sento col piede la terra, e tutta la
vita m'è chiara.

Ora posso vestirmi di foglie, e ridere e
piangere, leggera, col vento:

vestirmi di nube, e rincorrere, sotto la luna,
i cirri d'argento.

Riconoscere il volto mio vero in gocce di
pioggia, in gocce di luce:

essere, o uomo, il pane che mangi, la
speranza che ti conduce.

Salutarti col Verbo divino, braccio che zappi,
seno che allatti, bocca che canti,

casa che sorgi; e passar oltre, col passo lungo
dei camminanti.

Mirages

The Secret

I kissed a berry of the cypress, in the shade
  of the cypress grove:

joyful at the kiss, the fawn-colored berry gave
  me a secret.

Now, as I lock the secret of the trees in my
  bittersweet mouth,

I no longer feel the earth under my feet, and all
  of life is clear.

Now, I can dress myself with leaves, and laugh
  and cry, light, with the wind:

dress myself with clouds, and chase, in the moonlight,
  the silver cirrus.

Recognize my true face in beads of rain, in beads
  of light:

to be, o man, the bread you eat, the hope
  that guides you.

Greet you with the divine Word: arm that digs,
  breast that nurses, mouth that sings,

house that rises; and go past, with the long
  step of those who keep walking.

Filastrocca

*Sette fiammelle di barche, che vanno a
   pescare:*
l'Orsa Maggiore è caduta, è caduta nel mare.
L'Orsa Maggiore cammina nel chiaro di luna
lungo i sentieri dell'acque cercando fortuna.
*"Sette fiammelle dell'Orsa, che andate a
   cercare?"*
*"Donna, cerchiamo un fanciullo perduto
   nel mare.*
Forse non è più nel mare, è nella montagna:
*forse a quest'ora dorme, all'ombra di
   Matermagna.*
Noi chiederem la sua grazia alle bianche Sirene:
*come può viver la madre che ha perso il suo
   bene?"*
*"Se quel fanciullo trovate per cale o per
   grotte*
vi darò tutte le rose sbocciate stanotte:
*vi darò tutte le perle che in grembo alle
   foglie*
fino al mattino la fresca rugiada raccoglie:
vi tesserò col mio canto la magica via
che vi riadduca fra gli astri, lassù in compagnia."

*Sette fiammelle di barche che vanno a
   pescare:*
l'Orsa Maggiore è caduta, è caduta nel mare.

Nursery Rhyme

Like little flames, seven boats out to fish
   in the sea:

the Big Dipper has fallen, fallen into the sea.

The Big Dipper travels in the light of the moon

along trails of waters in search of good fortune.

"Seven flames of the Dipper, what are you
   after?"

"Woman, we search for a youth who was lost
   in the waters.

Perhaps he's no longer in the sea, he's in the mountain:

maybe he sleeps at this hour, in the shade
   of Great Mother.

We will ask the white Mermaids to spare him:

for how can a mother who lost her beloved
   keep living?"

"If you find that young boy in a cove or
   a cavern

I will give you all the roses that blossomed tonight:

I will give you all the pearls the fresh dew
   collects

until morning in a bosom of leaves:

for you I will weave a magic path with my song

to lead you back to the stars, up there among them."

Like little flames, seven boats out to fish
   in the sea:

the Big Dipper has fallen, fallen into the sea.

La tessitrice

Tessitrice, che in ordine lento le sete e i
  colori disponi al telaio

augusto — e ti veglian le rocce, e ti fa
  òmbra un rosaio:

che a intrider di sole e di luna le tele sulla
  riva dei naufraghi adduci

e riadduci la spola guizzante tra fili d'oro,
  fili di luce:

tessimi il drappo dell'ultimo sogno, tessilo
  saldo, tessilo bene,

che vi sia dentro, tramato in porpora, tutto
  l'intrico delle mie vene.

Tessilo di risa, tessilo di pianti, e di quel
  nome che in cuore ho sepolto:

ch'esso mi vesta sin quando io viva, che
  morte mi copra il volto.

The Weaver

Weaver, slowly you arrange your silks and colors
  on your stately loom

— and the rocks watch over you,
  a rosebush shades you:

and to infuse your cloths of the sun and the moon
  on the shore of the shipwrecked,

you dart your spool back and forth
  between threads of gold, threads of light:

weave me a cloth of the last dream; weave it
  taut, weave it well,

so that in it, woven in crimson, is the whole
  tangle of my veins.

Weave it with laughter, weave it with tears,
  and with the name I have buried in my heart:

so it may clothe me as long as I live, so that
  death may cover my face.

Miraggi

Non eran che vani fantasmi, sospesi nel vuoto,
   le rupi sireniche,

e sotto il piede non terra, non pietra, ma
   aerea sostanza di nube.

Bianchi vapori, polvere d'astri, ondeggiarono
   intorno alla luna,

formando e sfacendo ali e tuniche d'angeli,
   sideree scale,

reggie di sogno: d'esse, nel pallido incanto,
   io regina, voi re.

MIRAGES

The cliffs of the mermaids, suspended in void,
 were no more than vain phantoms,

with no ground, no rock, underfoot, only
 the ethereal essence of clouds.

White vapors, astral dust, were swaying
 around the moon,

making and unmaking wings and tunics of angels,
 stairs of stars,

palaces of dreams; of them, in that pale enchantment,
 I was queen, you were king.

La roccia

O roseodorata!...Dove mai vidi sì piena, sì
fulgida carne?

Non oso sfiorarti, per tema d'una pronta
vendetta del sole.

Tu respiri: l'amplesso del sole ti riga di
brividi lunghi,

e nessun volto di donna, riverso nel bacio,
ardendo e godendo sorride

come te, roccia del Monte Solaro, amante
amata.

The Rock

O rose-scented one! Where did I
　　ever see such full, such radiant flesh?

I dare not touch you, for fear of the sun's quick
　　revenge.

You breathe: the sun embraces you
　　in long shivering strokes,

and no woman's face, leaning back in a kiss,
　　burning with pleasure, smiles

like you, rock of Mount Solaro, beloved
　　lover.

La spiaggia delle vedove

Così voi raccontaste, ed io tremai nell'udire,

mentre la voce marina, rompente agli scogli,
diceva di sì.

(C'era una gioia e un tormento in quell'andare
e venire

dell'onde: una gioia e un tormento in quel
dire di sì.)

"Da questa spiaggia, nel tempo lontano,
all'alba d'un limpido giorno,

i pescatori di Capri partirono a pesca, per
lieto ritorno.

Ma un loro pianto nascosto piangevan le
donne accanto alle cune,

accendendo la pia candeletta alla Madonna
delle Fortune.

La notte, i marosi assaltarono il cielo, il cielo
piombò dentro l'acque:

e fin che non ebbe l'ultimo uomo, non risalì
il cielo, il mare non giacque.

Qui calaron le vedove, in torma, clamando,
imprecando al cielo ed al mare:

poi — coi giorni — ripreser, placate, a tender

The Widows' Beach

Here's how you told it, and I trembled
    to hear it,

while the voice of the sea, breaking against
    the cliffs, said yes.

(There was a joy and a torment, in that coming
    and going

of waves: a joy and a torment in that saying
    yes.)

"From this beach, long ago, on the dawn
    of a clear day,

the fishermen of Capri set out to fish, sure
    of a happy return.

But, next to the cradles, their women were crying
    hidden tears,

lighting a small pious candle to Our Lady
    of Fates.

That night, the breakers assaulted the sky, the sky
    plunged into the waters:

and not until the last man was taken, did the sky
    re-ascend, did the sea lie at rest.

Here, the widows came down in throngs, clamoring,
    cursing the sky and the sea:

then — as days passed — placated, they resumed

le reti, cucire, filare.

Non vi spiaccia: ché sempre una barca vi
    sarà che a una secca si schianta:

sempre, a riva, una donna (gran festa di
    schiume, oggi, al sole!) che piange, poi
    canta."

Così voi raccontaste, ed io tremai nell'udire,

mentre la voce marina, rompente agli scogli,
    diceva di sì.

(C'era una gioia e un tormento in quell'andare
    e venire

dell'onde: una gioia e un tormento in quel
    dire di sì.)

the tending of nets, the sewing, the spinning.

Don't be sad: there will always be a boat
   that breaks on a shoal:

always, on shore, a woman (what a feast
   of sea-foam, today, in the sun!) who weeps,
   and then sings.

Here's how you told it, and I trembled
   to hear it,

while the voice of the sea, crashing against
   the cliffs, said yes.

(There was a joy and a torment, in that coming
   and going

of waves: a joy and a torment in that saying
   yes.)

Torre Saracena

Alta la scalinata di Torre Saracena

nel mio ricordo, fra il cielo e il mare antico.

Il mare antico dei naufraghi canta e si rompe
    d'amore

contro la scalinata di Torre Saracena

che non l'ascolta; ma ascolta divine parole
    dal cielo.

Alta la scalinata di Torre Saracena:

vi ascende, fra due azzurri, la mia felicità.

SARACEN TOWER

High is the stairway of Saracen Tower,

in my memory, between the sky and the ancient sea.

The ancient sea of castaways sings and shatters
   with love

against the stairway of Saracen Tower

that doesn't listen; though it listens to divine
   words from the sky.

High is the stairway of Saracen Tower:

there, between two blues, ascends my happiness.

✺ Scirocco

Non so che livido volto mi mostri oggi
  Monte Tiberio,

inciso di cicatrici, saturo d'odio, forse
  d'amore:

il volto di colui che fu per uccidermi, un
  giorno.

Ov'è colui che un giorno fu per uccidermi,
  perché mi amava?

Ch'io tremi ancora al suo fiato geloso, ch'io
  svenga in quel brivido.

Carcere duro è l'Isola ov'io mi credetti aria
  ed ala:

l'alte rocce son mura di mastio, impervie:
  sul mare cinereo

non onda, non vela, non varco, non remissione:
  e pur sento,

malfida Capri, ch'è dolce, troppo dolce esser
  vinta da te.

Sirocco

I do not know the livid face you're showing me today
  Mount Tiberius,

marked with scars, filled with hate, maybe
  with love:

the face of him who was about to kill me,
  one day.

Where is he, who one day was about to kill me,
  because he loved me?

That I may tremble still in his jealous breath, that I
  may faint in that shiver.

The Island where I believed I was air and wing
  is a harsh prison:

the high rocks are the walls of a fortress, impassable:
  on the ash-colored sea

no wave, no sail, no opening, no escape: and yet
  I feel that,

deceitful Capri, it's sweet, too sweet to be
  conquered by you.

Maestrale

So che domani riderai, perduta
  nell'azzurra follia del maestrale.

Così ignuda sarai, che i tuoi roseti
  segneranno le vie delle tue vene.

Riderai come donna innamorata
  sotto il crosciar frenetico dei baci.

Saliran fino al cielo le tue risa,
  fino alle grotte s'inabisseranno.

Grotta Meravigliosa, Grotta Azzurra,
  Grotta di Matermagna, Grotta Verde,

solchi scavati dalla passione
  del mare nella tua carne di luce:

ch'io mi distempri in luce, ch'io non sia
  che un barbaglio di gocciole nel sole,

e in ogni goccia l'universo viva!

MISTRAL

I know that tomorrow you will laugh, lost
   in the mistral's blue folly.

You'll be so naked, your rose beds
   will show the paths of your veins.

You will laugh like a woman in love
   under a frenzied shower of kisses.

Your laughter will rise to the sky,
   it will plunge deep in the caves.

Grotto of Wonders, Blue Grotto,
   Grotto of Great Mother, Green Grotto,

gullies dug by the passion
   of the sea into your flesh made of light:

that I may melt in this light, that I may be
   no more than a dazzle of drops in the sun,

and may the universe live in each drop!

Ulivi

☀ LA SOFFERENZA

Non credevi soffrire così, donna, ancora
   così,

col torbido cuore pesante entro il torbido
   corpo.

Con la certezza che il male è senza rimedio,
   e quasi ne godi.

Con lo spavento che altri lo sappia, e ti possa
   irridere.

Oh, tanta vergogna ne avresti, che meglio esser
   morta.

Ma — donna — orgoglio è in te di soffrire
   ancora così,

perchè un tale dolore è dolore di giovinezza:

e tu sei pronta alla morte: alla rinunzia, no.

Olive Trees

✺ Suffering

You didn't believe you'd be suffering like this,
 woman, still like this,

with a troubled heart heavy inside a turbid
 body.

With the certainty that such pain is without cure,
 you almost take joy in it.

With the dread that others may know,
 and mock you.

Oh, you would feel such shame, you would
 rather die.

Yet — woman — within you is the pride to suffer
 still,

since such ache is the ache of youth:

and you are ready for death: not defeat.

L'ULIVETO

Pallidi son gli ulivi dell'uliveto al monte:

a ognuno ho dato un nome e a quel nome risponde:

nel mezzo sta il più grande e tutto sa di me.

Tutto di me gli dissi, un vespro che la luna

sorgeva, tonda e pura come l'ostia eucaristica,

dal mare immoto; e tanto piansi, che da ogni lacrima

sbocciò per compassione una tenera foglia.

Tenere foglie, trame di perla, succhi d'anima,

voglio ascoltar quest'oggi la vostra aerea musica.

Voglio dormire all'ombra di tutte le mie lacrime:

oh, così chiara: velo d'argento, ombra di nuvola.

Ulivo, padre ulivo: tu mi vedi: non posso

viver così, di nulla: di nessuno, senza nessuno,

senza amar, senza odiare, non più serva, non più donna.

The Olive Grove

The olive trees in the mountain grove are pale:

I've given each one a name and to that name
   it replies:

the largest one, in the middle, knows everything about me.

I told it everything about me, on an evening the moon
   rose round and pure, like a Eucharistic host,

from the motionless sea; and I wept so, that from
   each tear

a tender leaf bloomed in compassion.

Tender leaves, wefts of pearl, soul's essence,

on this day, I want to listen to your aerial
   music.

I want to sleep in the shade of all my
   tears:

oh, so clear: veil of silver, hint of
   cloud.

Olive tree, father tree: you see me: I cannot

live this way, on nothing: of no one,
   with no one,

without loving, without hating, no longer servant,
   no longer woman.

Tu lo sai: se ho peccato, fu per amore: or
dimmi

tu la parola estrema che ancor mi sia
d'amore,

e ch'io ti muoia ai piedi: raccoglimi tu,
padre:

fammi radice in terra ch'è tua, linfa nel
tronco.

Voglio dormire all'ombra di tutte le mie
lacrime:

tenue ombra, e senza viso come l'oblìo:
suprema

grazia, l'oblìo: clemenza suprema, ombra
di Dio.

You know this: if I've sinned, it was for love: now
   you tell me

the final word that may yet be
   of love,

and that I may die at your feet: receive me,
   father:

make me a root in your soil, lymph
   in your body.

I want to sleep in the shade of all my
   tears:

a tenuous shade with no face, like oblivion:
   supreme

grace, oblivion: supreme mercy, shade
   of God.

IL PAESE

*Fra gli ulivi, fra gli ulivi, in un giorno di
   nostalgia,*

*con le sorgenti del pianto il mio paese
   rinacque in me.*

*Dissi al cuore: "Del dolce paese conviene
   riprender la via:*

*cuore ch'è in terra lontana cuore vivente
   non è."*

※

*Ma gli ulivi, ma gli ulivi, con cenni di braccia
   paterne,*

*con murmure buono di fronde mi chiesero
   in coro: "Perché?*

*Scava nel suolo, e cerca del paese le radici
   eterne*

*dovunque è un'ombra d'albero che si raccolga
   su te."*

The Village

Among the olive trees, among the olive trees,
   on a day of nostalgia,

with springs of tears, my village was reborn
   in me.

I said to my heart: "Better take the road to the sweet
   village again:

a heart in a distant land is a heart no longer
   living."

But the olive trees, but the olive trees, with a wave
   of their fatherly arms,

with a kindly murmur of foliage, asked me,
   in chorus: "What for?

Dig deep in the soil, and look for the eternal roots
   of your village

wherever there's the shade of a tree that gathers
   you in."

NOSTALGIE

☀ CASA DÒMINA

ALLA MEMORIA DI LUISA VISMARA

Dama Luisa, che alla mia lontana
adolescenza così dolce fosti
che la dolcezza avea sentor di fiori:
e quando a te mi tolsero le vie
del mondo, sempre in cuore ebbi fragrante
quella dolcezza, e mi durò la voce
grave, d'organo, in fondo alla memoria:
dopo tant'anni, ti ritrovo: dolce
qual eri, e solo un po' più curva: nella
casa romita che somiglia un'ala
sospesa sulla libertà del mare.

Qui, per la gioia de' tuoi anni estremi,
ti condusse per mano il buon figliuolo:
quegli che più degli altri amasti, e pure
tutti eran cari al faticato grembo:
quegli che un giorno, nelle umili stanze
ch'or sembran di leggenda, in Santa Marta,
strano fanciullo solo in te perduto,
t'adorava, in ginocchio; e adesso, forte
tra i forti, bimbo è nel tuo bacio ancora:
ché tu, per lui, morta non sei; ma resti
soave in Casa Dòmina custode.

Occhiserena sotto la cuffietta
nera, di trina, e i ferri tra le dita
che mai del saggio oprar furono stanche,
mi guardi; ma non mi ravvisi più.
Foschi, allora, i capelli, come grappoli
di mirtillo: ricordi?...e lampeggiante
di giovinezza il volto. Oh, tanto piangere,
sai, da quel tempo; e tanto errare, e tanto

Nostalgia

Casa Dòmina

In memory of Luisa Vismara

Dame Luisa, in my distant
youth you were so sweet
your sweetness had the scent of flowers:
and when life's path took me away from you,
in my heart I always felt the fragrance
of that sweetness, and your voice, grave
as an organ's, stayed deep in my memory.
After many years, I find you again—sweet
as you were, just a little more bent—
in the remote house that resembles a wing
suspended above the freedom of the sea.

Here, to enjoy your final years,
your good son led you by the hand:
he whom you loved more than the others, though
they were all dear to your tired womb:
he who, once —in the humble rooms
in Saint Marta, now like a legend—
was an odd child devoted solely to you,
adored you, on his knees; and now, though strong
as any man, in your kiss he's still a boy:
because to him, you are not dead, but remain
the gentle keeper of Casa Dòmina.

Eyes serene beneath a little black
bonnet of lace, knitting needles in your fingers,
never tiring of sensible work,
you look at me; but no longer recognize me.
Once, your hair was dark like a cluster
of myrtle, remember? And your face
sparkled with youth. Oh, so many tears,
you know, since that time; so many mistakes,

*offendere la vita ch'è sì bella
e grande; ed ecco, ora son qui. Non dirmi
nulla: tutto è ormai detto, ed è compiuto.*

*Ma non io sola cercherò la pace
e un rinnovato albor d'infanzia nella
tua carezza, o beata. Altri verranno.
Verranno a Casa Dòmina in Tragara,
rifugio estremo, i naufraghi del sogno,
com'io già venni, dalle tristi rive.
Affranti; e qui ritroveran la vita.
Orfani; e qui ritroveran la madre.
Per il lungo tormento e il pianto vano
ciechi nel cuore; e dal tuo cuore assunti
alla luce che vince ogni altra luce.*

E sarà il mare un prato d'asfodèli.

and so many sins against life so great
and beautiful; and here I am. Say
nothing: all has been said by now, and done.

But I won't be alone looking for peace
and a renewed glimmer of childhood
in your caress, o blessed one. Others will come.
They, the castaways of dreams, will come
as I did, from unhappy shores
to Casa Dòmina in Tragara, the final refuge.
Downtrodden, here they will find life again.
Orphans, here they will find a mother again.
Blind in their hearts through long suffering
and useless weeping, they are taken into
your heart to a light brighter than any other.

And the sea will be a meadow of asphodels.

Lettera a Bianca

*Oh, tu, figlia! Oh, tanta terra e tanto mare
fra noi!*

*Quando fu mai, fra noi, tanta terra e tanto
mare?*

*E come puoi vivere senza di me? Dimmi
che non puoi!*

*Saprò forse allora strapparmi all'incanto,
lasciare*

*l'Isola dolce. So, ch'essa è sogno: ch'è vana
parvenza*

di sogno. Sparire potrebbe, così, all'improvviso,

*nei flutti, o nel gorgo solare; e, con essa, la
mia demenza...*

*Serro sugli occhi le mani, per salvarmi; e nel
cuor ti ravviso.*

*Sei sulla terrazza, in tunica bianca: allatti la
tua Donatella.*

*Sole velato su lei, su te, attraverso le grappe
e le fronde*

*del glicine. Vien da San Barnaba, ingenuo,
un canto di campanella:*

*letizia materna ti penetra col succhiar della
bimba, a grandi onde.*

Letter to Bianca

You, oh daughter! Oh, so much land and so much sea
between us!

When was there ever, between us, so much land and so much
sea?

And how can you live without me? Tell me you can't!

Perhaps then I'll know how to wrench myself from this spell,
leave

this sweet Island I know is a dream: a vain
semblance

of a dream. It could vanish, like that, all at once,

in the waves, or in a vortex of sun; and, with it,
my dementia…

I press my eyes shut with my hands to save myself;
and I see you again in my heart.

You're in a white tunic, on the terrace, nursing
your Donatella.

The sun veiled over her, over you, through clusters
and fronds

of wisteria. The innocent song of a small bell comes
from Saint Barnabas:

the child's suckling sends great waves of maternal
bliss through you.

Altro non sai, nè chiedi. Ti basta la tua
verità.

Ala fanno i capelli sul volto, perduto nel volto
che gli somiglia.

Raccolgono gli occhi la luce del cielo sulla
diletta, che gode e non sa.

Così, in cuore, ti penso — e mi salvo, — giovine
madre che sei la mia figlia.

You know nothing else, nor do you ask. Your truth
  is enough.

Your hair falls like a wing over your face, lost
  in the face that resembles it.

Your eyes gather light from the sky upon
  your beloved who, unknowing, takes pleasure.

Thus, in my heart, I think of you — and save myself —
  young mother, daughter of mine.

Lettera a Bianca

Tornerò: non temere: quando l'ebbrezza
sarà caduta.

Tutto cade: il fiore ed il frutto, la bacca
e la ghianda.

Tutto ritorna: l'ala alla terra, la barca alla
riva.

Mi rivedrà la casa ove tenta i suoi primi
gorgheggi Donata,

ove Mikika ronfa, vibrando il dorso arcuato
sugli embrici al sole.

Lasciami vivere, adesso — ché breve è il
mio tempo — negli orti d'oro.

Viva forse non fui, se non ora: né pur
quando i fianchi

tu mi rompesti nascendo, e fosti la mia
primavera.

Un altro maggio è qui, che ignoravo
splendesse nel mondo.

Dio m'ha condotta negli alti luoghi: che in
essi io m'esalti

di me: ch'io tocchi le cime: ch'io beva alle
fontane azzurre.

Ch'io mi vesta tutta di rose, e dia sangue
d'amore alle spine.

Letter to Bianca

I will return: do not fear: when my elation
   falls.

Everything falls: the flower and the fruit, the berry
   and the acorn.

Everything returns: the wing to the earth, the boat
   to the shore.

The house where Donata attempts her first sounds
   will see me again,

where Mikika purrs, vibrating his arched back
   on the sun-warmed tiles.

Right now, let me live — since my time is brief —
   amid golden orchards.

Perhaps I was never alive, until now: not even
   when at birth

you burst open my hips, and you were my
   spring.

Here is another May, whose splendor upon the world
   I used to ignore.

God has led me to high places: that in them
   I, too, may rise:

that I may touch the summits: that I may drink
   from blue fountains.

That I may dress all of me with roses, and give
   their thorns the blood of love.

*Un giorno, chi sa?...nell'anima stanca mi
  pungerà desiderio*

*d'un campo arato di Lombardia, fresco di
  solchi, fumante e bruno*

*nella nebbia filtrata di sole: allora al paese
  verrò,*

*per ritrovarti verrò, bruna e feconda come
  quel campo.*

One day, who knows? My tired soul may be
  pierced with desire

for a plowed field of Lombardy, its ditches fresh,
  steaming, and dark

in the filtered haze of the sun: then I will come
  to the village,

I will come to find you again, dark and fertile
  like that field.

Le Strade

E s'io non tornassi? — Lontana da me, fra
 siepi di fior d'ogni mese

serena tu andrai dove il giovine amore ti
 chiama,

con Donatella al fianco, e tu al fianco dell'uomo
 in cui guardi.

Due volte alle madri è reciso, per legge di
 vita, il cordone del sacro umbilìco:

nel travaglio glorioso del parto, e dopo
 vent'anni.

Diverse sono le strade, se pur uno ed uguale
 è l'amore,

figlia; ma sempre al mio pianto tu sei quella
 che in grembo nascosta

per nove mesi io tenni; e baciavo la carne
 mia dolce, per te baciare;

e di nessuno tu eri — né pur del tuo padre —
 solo eri di me.

The Roads

And if I don't return? Far from me, you will go
 serene among each month's

hedgerows of flowers, to where your young love
 calls,

Donatella by your side, and you by the side
 of the man you gaze upon.

By life's decree, a mother's sacred umbilicus
 is severed twice:

in the glorious labor of childbirth, and twenty
 years later.

The roads are different, although love's path
 is one and the same,

daughter; yet, in my grief, you are forever the one
 I held, concealed in my womb,

for nine months; and I kissed my soft skin
 to kiss you;

and you were of no one — not even your father —
 you were only of me.

Canzone bretone

"Canta, streghetta." Così
pregava; e tu, coi fili
della tua voce, coi fili
de' suoi capelli
tessevi una rete d'incanto:
immerse le dita sottili
nei riccioli, come su corde
d'arpa a quei brividi
lunghi ritmavi il tuo canto.

Era un antico canto
della Bretagna, intriso
di salsedini marine
e di lacrime senza fine,
una nenia di culla
e di bara. — Tutto e nulla.

Bassa e calda la voce
come una confessione,
a ad ogni nota più pallido
il viso, e più addentro le dita
nelle dorate chiome:
canto oscuro, simile a te,
modulato a ninna-nanna
sul capo dell'adolescente
più bello del figlio del re.

...Streghetta, quel tempo è passato.
Lungi dorme l'adolescente
ch'era più bello del figlio del re.
Niun destare può il dormiente,
ché eterno è il sonno sovra il Col d'Èchele.
Grumi di sangue fra i bei capelli.
Grumi di pianto nella canzone
che più non canti (io sola
quel tempo ricordo, e la voce
bassa e calda, di confessione):

"Dors, mon petit gas..."

Breton Song

Sing, little sorceress. Thus
she prayed; and you, with the threads
of your voice, with the threads
of his hair
wove a net of enchantment:
your slender fingers immersed
in his curls, as if on the strings
of a harp, to those long shivers
the rhythm of your song...

It was an ancient song
of Brittany, steeped
in the salt of the sea
and in tears without end,
a chant for the cradle
and the coffin — everything and nothing.

The voice was low and warm,
like a confession,
and at each note your face
grew paler, your fingers
deeper in the golden locks:
a dark song, like you,
adapted to a lullaby
above the head of the youth
more beautiful than the son of the king.

...Little sorceress, that time is past.
Long sleeps the youth more beautiful
than the son of the king.
No one can awaken him,
for atop Mount Echele sleep is eternal.
Clots of blood in his beautiful hair.
Clots of tears in the song
you no longer sing (I alone
remember that time, and your voice
low and warm, as in confession):

"Dors, mon petit gas(con)..."

Ada Negri

Ritorno
per il dolce Natale

Disse la madre: "Lasciate socchiusa la porta
ch'egli verrà."

Fu lasciata socchiusa la porta: egli entra,
disceso dall'eternità.

Per strade di neve e di fango gli fu guida la
stella in cammino

nei cieli sol quando rinasce, dentro una stalla,
Gesù Bambino.

Riaccosta l'uscio in silenzio, appende in
silenzio al gancio il mantello

(fori e bruciacchi di shrapnel nella divisa
ridotta un brandello):

ma ben calca sugli occhi l'elmetto, che la
fronte non sia veduta,

e siede, al suo posto, nel cerchio della
famiglia pallida e muta.

"Mamma, perchè non ti vedo la veste di
seta dal gaio colore?"

" È in fondo all'armadio, è in fondo all'armadio:
domani la metto, mio dolce amore."

"Babbo, perchè cosi curvo, perchè tante
rughe intorno ai tuoi occhi?"

"Son vecchio, ormai: vecchio e stanco; ma

Return
for Sweet Christmas

Said the mother: "Leave the door ajar
   for he will come."

The door was left ajar: he enters,
   descended from eternity.

Through streets of snow and mud, he is guided
   by a star on his journey

from heaven only when Baby Jesus is born
   again in a stable.

He closes the door in silence, in silence he hangs
   his cloak on a hook

(holes and burn-marks of shrapnel in his uniform
   torn to shreds)

but he pulls his helmet down, over his eyes, so no one
   can see his forehead,

and he sits, at his place, in the circle of the family
   pale and mute.

"Mother, why don't I see you in your silk dress
   of bright color?"

"It's deep in the wardrobe, it's deep in the wardrobe:
   I'll wear it tomorrow, my sweet love."

"Father, why so bent, why so many
   lines around your eyes?"

"I'm old, by now: old and tired; but all will pass,

tutto passa, se tu mi tocchi."

"Sorellina dal piede leggero, perchè un nastro
nero fra i riccioli biondi?"

"T'inganni, ha il color del cielo, ha il colore
dei mari profondi."

Intanto, dalle campane della messa di
mezzanotte

gigli e gigli di pace e d'amore fioriranno nella
santa notte.

Ed ecco al "Gloria" drizzarsi nell'alta e sottile
persona il soldato,

togliendo dal capo l'elmetto, piamente, con
gesto pacato.

Scoperta arderà in mezzo al fronte l'ampia
stimmate sanguinosa:

corona di re consacrato, fiamma eterna,
divina rosa.

Ma sotto il diadema del sangue egli il capo
reclinerà

come chi nulla ha dato, come chi nulla avrà.

if you touch me."

"Little sister with the light step, why a black
ribbon in your fair curls?"

"You're mistaken, it's the color of sky, it's the color
of deep seas."

Meanwhile, from the bells of midnight
mass,

lilies upon lilies of peace and of love bloom
in the holy night.

And at the "*Gloria*," the soldier stands,
erect in his tall slender figure,

removing the helmet from his head, piously,
with placid gesture.

Uncovered, in the center of his brow,
glows his wide bloody stigmata:

crown of an anointed king, eternal flame,
divine rose.

Yet beneath the diadem of blood, he lowers
his head

like one who has given nothing, like one
who will have nothing.

Donata

*Bimba, che entrando nel mondo svelasti a
tua madre la vita-vivente*

*com'ella a me, nel tempo in cui ero, più che
anima, carne:*

*non somigliano ai nostri i tuoi occhi, color
degli stagni nell'ombra:*

*altro è l'arco della tua fronte, altro il segno
del tuo futuro.*

*E pure io so che un giorno ti splenderà in
bocca il mio riso ventenne*

*e, in un gesto, in un bacio, in un balzo di
chiaro odio, di chiaro amore,*

*nello zampillo d'un canto risarai la fanciulla
ch'io fui.*

*Forse l'opera bella che chiusa restò in me,
mal viva, mal morta,*

*tu compirai nel sole, per alta sapienza di
Nostro Signore.*

*Così la mia madre gaudiosa passò nelle vene
a tua madre:*

*in te, così, mi prolungo: e tu, quando giusto
sia il punto,*

*ne' tuoi figli e ne' figli dei figli: e niun seme
verrà trascurato*

*e niuna forza dispersa; e chi muore vivrà;
e in questa certezza ti amo*

*dell'amore che va dal principio sino all'ultima
discendenza.*

DONATA

Child, upon entering this world, you revealed
   to your mother the living-life

as she did to me, at the time when I was flesh
   more than spirit,:

your eyes, the color of ponds in the shade, do not
   resemble ours:

the arch of your brow is different, the mark
   of your future is different.

And yet, I know, the smile I had at twenty
   will shine on your lips one day

and, in a gesture, in a kiss, in a leap of sheer hate,
   of sheer love,

in the gush of a song, you will be the girl
   I once was.

Maybe, by the mighty wisdom of Our Lord,
   you will bring into sunlight

the great work that stayed locked inside me,
   barely living, barely dying.

Thus, my joyous mother continued through the veins
   of your mother:

and so in you, I live on: and you, when the moment
   is right,

in your children and in their children's children: and no seed
   will be neglected

and no force dispersed; and whoever dies shall live;
   and in this certainty I love you

with a love that goes from the first to the last
   line of descent.

Il sagrato

*Il gran corale del luglio sale in clangori di
   trombe d'oro*

*a tua gloria; ed il mare ti cinge di fiamme,
   o tirrenia Valchiria.*

*Io chiudo gli occhi; e penso, fra campi di lino
   turchino,*

*grave di pianti d'organo, un sagrato di
   chiesa lombarda.*

*Ombra gli fanno i platani, fresca l'erba gli
   ride fra i sassi:*

*la neve d'inverno lo ammanta d'immacolata
   pace.*

The Churchyard

The grand chorale of July rises in a blare
   of gold trumpets

to your glory; and the sea girds you in flames,
   o Tyrrhenian Valkyrie.

I close my eyes; and think of a Lombard churchyard,
   among flax fields

of deep-blue, heavy from the organ's weeping.

The sycamore trees give it shade, the cool grass
   smiles at it from amid its stones:

the winter snow cloaks it in immaculate
   peace.

LONTANO

Nel ricordo, nel desiderio, un tetto rosso,
un lastrico grigio, lucenti di pioggia.

Dolce pioggia senza vento, dolce brusire sul
tetto e sul lastrico.

Oltre il tetto, la cima d'un olmo gorgheggia
per stormi di passeri

che senton vicina la sera; e tu ignori, tu ignori
qual sia

più lontano, più caro e più triste al tuo male
di nostalgia,

se il brusir della pioggia sugli embrici o il
gorgheggio rissoso dei passeri.

Away

In remembrance, in desire, a red rooftop,
  a gray pavement, shining with rain.

Gentle rain without wind, gentle rustle
  on rooftop and pavement.

Beyond the rooftop, the tip of an elm trills
  with flocks of sparrows

who feel the evening draw near; and you don't know,
  you don't know which

is more distant, more dear and more sad to your ache
  of nostalgia,

whether the rustle of rain on the roof-tiles
  or the quarrelsome trill of the sparrows.

Il mandorlo

C'era un mandorlo, che fioriva
ogni aprile, in un orto ch'io so.
Quando era tutto un biancore,
le nubi, dall'alto, pensavano
che una d'esse fosse caduta.

Intorno, case di poveri
con logge garrule, e stracci
appesi ai ferri; e un gran ridere
nei cortiletti, di bimbi;
e suonar d'organetti, al crocicchio.

Contar volli i fiori del mandorlo
una volta (ero innamorata).
Ma forse si contano i bimbi
dei poveri, i baci, le stelle
del cielo, le gocce di pioggia?

Morto è l'albero di giovinezza
e sta per morire il mio cuore.
O aprile, non fare ritorno:
vano è il tuo ritorno, se chiusi
per sempre son gli occhi del mandorlo.

The Almond Tree

There was an almond tree that bloomed
each April, in an orchard I know.
When all of it was whiteness,
the clouds, from above, thought
one of them had fallen.

All around, homes of the poor
with noisy balconies, rags
hanging on clothes-lines; the great laughter
of children in the small courtyards;
the sound of barrel organs at the crossroads.

Once, I wanted to count the blossoms
of the almond tree (for I was in love).
But, can the children of the poor,
kisses, stars in the sky,
raindrops, be counted?

The tree of youth is dead
and my heart is about to die.
O April, do not return:
your return is in vain, if the eyes
of the almond tree are closed forever.

Un sogno

Leggero, il sonno mi portò lontano.
Così lontano, ch'io non seppi più
ove fossi: bianca era una strada
fra case basse, sotto nubi e nubi
grigio-moventi: senza nome e senza
fine la strada, e senza ore il tempo.

Ed aveva ogni casa un uscio aperto
su uno scalino; ma nessun sedeva
al limitare, e il vano era sì fosco
che mi parea la bocca d'una tomba;
ed il silenzio sì profondo, ch'io
pietra credetti essere ormai, fra pietre.

Ma camminavo; come si cammina
nei sogni, non staccando dalla terra
il piede. Ed ecco, sulla sesta soglia
un uomo apparve. E riconobbi il figlio
di mia madre in quell'uomo: il triste figlio
per cui tanto ella avea sofferto in cuore.

Disse: "Come ancor sei giovine e salda!
Ben, di noi, la più forte: tu, che hai nervi
d'acciaio, e bianco lampeggiar di denti
fra le quadre mascelle, e in te portasti
il coraggio senz'ombra e il sangue sano
di nostra madre, e il suo gioir di tutto.

Io fischiettavo al buio — ti ricordi? —
per non sentire il fiato della morte.
Annegavo nel vino — ti ricordi? —
la mia paura di morir trentenne.
Vegliavo in folli danze — ti ricordi? —
per lo spavento di spirar nel sonno.

A Dream

Lightly, sleep carried me far away.
So far away, I no longer knew
where I was: a white road
among low houses, beneath clouds
and clouds of gray — in motion: the road
had no name and no end, and time had no hours.

And each house had a door opening
onto a small step; but no one was sitting
on the threshold, and the entrance was so dark
it seemed to me the mouth of a tomb;
and the silence so deep that by then
I believed I was a stone among stones.

Yet I walked on; as one walks
in dreams, not taking my feet off
the earth. And there, on the sixth threshold,
a man appeared. And in that man
I recognized my mother's son: the unhappy
son she had suffered so much for.

He said: "How young and healthy you still are!
By far the strongest among us: you, with nerves
of steel, gleaming white teeth
in your square jaw, carried inside you
the courage and wholesome blood
of our mother, and her joy in everything.

I used to whistle in the dark — remember? —
not to hear the breathing of death.
In wine, I drowned — remember? —
my fear of dying at thirty.
I stayed up at foolish dances — remember?
— for fright of dying in my sleep.

E la madre dov'è? Non si sa nulla
qui, di chi vive e di chi muore. Ognuno
qui è solo, nella sua tenebra eterna.
Dov'è la madre? Non mi amava: amava
te. Ma vederla pur vorrei: perdono
chiederle, d'esser nato dal suo ventre.

Pensa la fredda casa in via dell'Orfane,
e l'orto incolto, e i boschi in riva all'Adda,
e i tuoi sogni di gloria, e i miei d'amore,
tu quasi donna, io quasi uomo, entrambi
assetati di mordere al gran frutto.
Ma quel ch'io colsi era già guasto. Ed ora,

ora, o sorella..." e più non poté dire:
un pianto irrefrenabile, un'angoscia
supplice e vana ebbe negli occhi. Ahimè,
che la morte per lui non era oblìo:
sovra un suo bene, a lui distolto innanzi
d'esser dato, in eterno egli piangeva.

Tesi le braccia; ma le tesi al vuoto.
Parlar tentai; ma non m'uscì la voce.
Quel doloroso volto ondeggiar vidi
qual di naufrago emerso a fior del flutto:
poscia oscurarsi, e scomparire; e tutto
scomparve— e gli occhi mi feriva il sole.

And where is Mother? We know nothing here,
of who's living and who's dying. Here, everyone
is alone in his eternal darkness.
Where is Mother? She didn't love me: she loved
you. But I still would like to see her — ask her
forgiveness for being born of her womb.

Think of the cold house on Orphan Street,
the untended orchard, the woods by Adda's bank,
your dreams of glory, and mine of love;
you almost a woman, I almost a man, both
thirsting for a bite of the great fruit.
But, the one I picked was already spoiled. And now,

now, o sister..." and he could say no more:
unstoppable tears, an anguish,
suppliant and vain, were in his eyes. Alas,
for him death was not oblivion:
over his loved one, taken before
being given to him, he wept for eternity.

I held out my arms; but they held emptiness.
I tried to speak; but my voice didn't come.
I saw that mournful face swaying
like someone shipwrecked surfacing on a wave:
then it darkened and vanished; and everything
vanished—and the sun was piercing my eyes.

I CAPELLI

Madre, tu mi chiamavi "mamma"
nella tua vecchiezza bambina.
Triste nome in tua bocca per me,
dolce come le cose sante.

A pettinare i tuoi capelli
non volevi che le mie mani:
candidi fili di purità,
tremavo, quasi, nell'intrecciarli.

Ma non osai, baciarli non osai
quando la morte ti rese sì bella
che tutto parve di te risplendere
intorno al letto della tua pace.

Come pesanti, ora, queste mie mani
sul tuo capo sì lievi, una volta.
Come pesanti, e pur così vuote,
madre — e niuno ti pettina più.

Your Hair

Mother, you, in old age a child,
  used to call me *"mamma."*
  For me, a sad name on your lips,
  but sweet as sacred things.

You wanted no hands but mine
  to comb your hair:
  white threads of purity,
  I trembled, almost, braiding.

But I didn't dare, I didn't dare kiss it
  when death made you so beautiful
  that everything seemed to glow of you
  around your bed of peace.

How heavy, now, these hands
  so light on your head, one time.
  How heavy, and yet so empty, Mother
  — and no one is combing your hair.

La fronte

La morte aveva paura
della tua fronte augusta.
Tempio di casti pensieri,
vetta di volontà.

Non la turbava un'ombra,
non la solcava una ruga,
non dal sole traeva fulgore,
ma dalla propria bianchezza viva.

Avea quattro volte vent'anni,
e l'innocenza degli astri
che sono eterni e pur nascere
sembrano, in cielo, ogni sera.

E fu senza morte che andasti,
o madre, verso la vita
durabile: una notte d'agosto
ch'era tutta un gran pianto di stelle.

Scendevano, lagrime d'angeli,
le stelle, per te ricondurre
ai divini silenzi: ove splende
sol chi in terra ebbe sete di Dio.

Non soffro per te. Nella vita
durabile, donde mi guardi,
so che un giorno, più vasta del tempo,
ritroverò la tua fronte.

Your Brow

Death feared
  your regal brow.
  Temple of chaste thoughts,
  summit of will.

Untroubled by shadows,
  un-furrowed by wrinkles,
  its radiance did not come from the sun,
  but from its own vibrant purity.

At four times twenty, your brow
  had the innocence of stars
  that, though eternal, seem born
  in the sky every night.

And it was without dying that you,
  Mother, went toward unending
  life: on a night in August
  that was all a great weeping of stars.

The stars, tears of angels, descended
  to lead you back
  to the divine silences — where only those
  who on earth thirsted for God can shine.

I do not grieve for you. In unending
  life, from where you watch over me,
  I know that one day I will find
  your brow again, vaster than time.

Nel paese di mia madre

Nel paese di mia madre

Nel paese di mia madre v'è un campo quadrato,
   cinto di gelsi.

Di là da quel campo altri campi quadrati,
   cinti di gelsi.

Roggie scorrenti vi sono, fra alti argini, dritte,
   e non si sa dove fanno a finire.

La terra s'allarga a misura del cielo, e non si
   sa dove vada a finire.

Nel paese di mia madre v'han ponti di nebbia,
   che il vespro solleva da placidi fiumi:

varca il sogno quei ponti di nebbia, mentre
   le rive si stellan di lumi.

Pioppi e betulle di tremula fronda accompagnan
   de l'acque il fluire:

quando ne' rami s'impigliano gli astri, in
   quella pace vorrei morire.

Nel paese di mia madre un basso tugurio
   sonnecchia sul limite della risaia

e ronzano mosche lucenti, ghiotte, intorno
   a un ammasso di concio.

Possanza di morte, possanza di vita, nell'odore
   del concio: ne gode

In the Village of My Mother

In the Village of my Mother

In the village of my mother, there is a square field,
enclosed by mulberry trees.

Beyond that field, more square fields,
enclosed by mulberry trees.

There are canals flowing straight between levees,
and no one knows where they go.

The land widens as broad as the sky, and no one
knows where it goes.

In the village of my mother, there are bridges of fog
the evening lifts from placid rivers:

dreams go across those bridges of fog
while the banks are stellar with lights.

Poplars and birches, with quivering foliage,
accompany the waters' flow:

when the stars are entangled in branches, I would
want to die in that glow.

In the village of my mother, a low hovel dozes
at the edge of the rice field,

and shiny flies buzz with greed around
a heap of manure.

The force of death, the force of life,
in the odor of dung: from it the land takes joy

la terra dall'humus profondo, sotto la vampa
d'agosto che immobile sta.

Nel paese di mia madre, quando il tramonto
s'insanguina obliquo sui prati,

vien da presso, vien da lontano una canzone
di lunga via:

la disser gli alari alle cune, gli aratri alle marre,
le biche all'aie fiorite di lucciole,

vecchia canzone di gente lombarda: "La
Violetta la vaaa la vaaaa…."

deep in its soil, beneath the steady blaze
  of August.

In the village of my mother, when the sunset,
  bloodstained, slants over meadows,

from near, from far, comes a long-traveled
  song:

the andirons sang it to the cradles, the ploughs to the hoes,
  the wheat stacks to the farmyards in bloom with fireflies,

the old song of the Lombard people: *La Violetta
  la va…la va…*

Corale notturno

*Quando sarò sepolta nel paese di mia
   madre,*

*là dove la bruma confonde i fertili solchi
   terrestri, coi solchi del cielo,*

*le rane ed i rospi dei fossi mi canteranno la
   nenia notturna.*

*Dagli acquitrini melmosi, filtrando fra il
   bianco umidor della luna,*

*in soavi cadenze di flauti, in tremolii lunghi
   di pianto sciogliendomi il cuore,*

*blandiranno il mio sonno, custodi della
   perenne malinconia.*

*Malinconia della patria, con sapore di terra
   bagnata e di grano maturo,*

*con quieto pudore di case ove accendon le
   madri pei figli la lampada al desco,*

*con fumo di tetti, ansare di fabbriche, radici
   dei vivi e dei morti,*

*a me verrà, con me dormirà, portata da canti
   di rane e di rospi,*

quando sarò sepolta nel paese di mia madre.

Night Chorus

When I am buried in the village
  of my mother,

there where the mist mingles the fertile
  furrows of earth with the furrows of sky,

the frogs and toads in the ditches will sing
  their nightly dirge to me.

From the muddy marshes, filtering through
  the white dampness of the moon,

in a soft cadence of flutes, in long quivers
  of grief melting my heart,

they will blandish my sleep, guardians
  of perpetual melancholy.

Melancholy for my homeland, with its taste
  of wet earth and ripe wheat,

with the quiet modesty of homes where mothers
  light a lamp on the dinner table for their children,

with the smoke of rooftops, the panting of factories, roots
  of the living and of the dead;

it will come to me, it will sleep with me, transported
  by songs of frogs and toads,

when I am buried in the village of my mother.

ADA NEGRI

First Line Index

ITALIAN

Ho male di luce, ho male di te, Capri solare	2
Chi fu mai, che dall'alto del muro mi gettò	4
Così basse le stelle sul capo, che par mi	6
Solaria, il vento del sud scrolla e devasta	8
Il mare, tuo re, magnifico amante, ti donò	10
Or cercherai riposo, sotto I carrubi: ché gli	12
Fra l'erbe dàn sangue i papaveri: raccoglierli	14
Se il libeccio trascina le nubi per I capelli, e	16
Per la strada rupestre scendevo, verso la	18
La luna scende in giardino per le scale	20
Contro la porta chiusa, grovigli di rose canine	22
Rose di porpora, ne ho piene le braccia	24
Passo passo m'accompagnate lungo i giardini	26
Nutrita di roccia, tu affondi nella roccia le	28
Ho un tulipano viola, d'un viola intenso	30
Quando l'estate fende le pietre su gl'irti	32
Dolce nella memoria, mattino di festa, che	34
Uomo dell'Isola, tu la tua casa hai costrutta	36
Viandante, se vai fino a Punta Tragara	40
Nell'alta Anacapri, sorrisa da lucenti vitiferi	42
Voce che mi chiami, che mi dici: "Svégliati"	44
Chiesi all'alba: "Per quale prodigio ti sei	46
La luna stilla un suo pianto d'oro nel mar	48
Sommesso gorgheggio d'uccelli, nell'ombra	50
Tu che ti levi affranta dal tuo letto senza	52
M'apparve stanotte una stella sì viva, sì	54
Baciai la coccola del cipresso, nell'ombra	56
Sette fiammelle di barche, che vanno a	58
Tessitrice, che in ordine lento le sete e i	60
Non eran che vani fantasmi, sospesi nel vuoto	62
O roseodorata!...Dove mai vidi sì piena, sì	64
Così voi raccontaste, ed io tremai nell'udire	66
Alta la scalinata di Torre Saracena	70
Non so che livido volto mi mostri oggi	72
So che domani riderai, perduta	74
Non credevi soffrire così, donna, ancora	76
Pallidi son gli ulivi dell'uliveto al monte	78
Fra gli ulivi, fra gli ulivi, in un giorno di	82
Dama Luisa, che alla mia lontana	84

Oh, tu, figlia! Oh, tanta terra e tanto mare	88
Tornerò: non temere: quando l'ebbrezza	92
E s'io non tornassi? — Lontana da me, fra	96
"Canta, streghetta." Così	98
Disse la madre: "Lasciate socchiusa la porta	100
Bimba, che entrando nel mondo svelasti a	104
Il gran corale del luglio sale in clangori di	106
Nel ricordo, nel desiderio, un tetto rosso	108
C'era un mandorlo, che fioriva	110
Leggero, il sonno mi portò lontano	112
Madre, tu mi chiamavi "mamma"	116
La morte aveva paura	118
Nel paese di mia madre v'è un campo quadrato	120
Quando sarò sepolta nel paese di mia	124

English

Light pains me; you pain me, luminous Capri	3
Who was it that, from atop the wall, threw me	5
So low are the stars above my head, it seems	7
Solaria, the south wind shakes and destroys	9
The sea, your king, magnificent lover	11
Now you will look for rest, under the carob-trees	13
Among grasses, the poppies shed blood	15
If the southwest wind drags the clouds by the hair	17
Going down the rocky road, toward	19
The moon descends on the garden down the steps	21
Against the closed door, snarls of dog roses	23
Purple roses, my arms are filled with them	25
Step by step, you accompany me along	27
Nourished by rock, in the rock you sink	29
I have a violet tulip, an intense violet	31
When summer cleaves the stones on the rugged	33
Sweet in my memory, a feast-day morning	35
Man of the Island, you built your house	37
Passerby, if you go as far as Tragara Point	41
In high Anacapri, graced by luminous	43
Voice that calls me, that tells me: *Awaken*	45
I asked dawn: "By what miracle did you	47
The moon sheds her golden tears into the	49
A low warble of birds in the palest	51
You, who rise exhausted from your bed without	53

Tonight a star appeared to me so vibrant	55
I kissed a berry of the cypress, in the shade	57
Like little flames, seven boats out to fish	59
Weaver, slowly you arrange your silks and colors	61
The cliffs of the mermaids, suspended in void	63
O rose-scented one! Where did I	65
Here's how you told it, and I trembled	67
High is the stairway of Saracen Tower	71
I do not know the livid face you're showing me today	73
I know that tomorrow you will laugh, lost	75
You didn't believe you'd be suffering like this	77
The olive trees in the mountain grove are pale	79
Among the olive trees, among the olive trees	83
Dame Luisa, in my distant	85
You, oh daughter! Oh, so much land and so much sea	89
I will return: do not fear: when my elation falls	93
And if I don't return? Far from me, you will go	97
Sing, little sorceress. Thus	99
Said the mother: "Leave the door ajar	101
Child, upon entering this world, you revealed	105
The grand chorale of July rises in a blare	107
In remembrance, in desire, a red rooftop	109
There was an almond tree that bloomed	111
Lightly, sleep carried me far away	113
Mother, you, in old age a child	117
Death feared	119
In the village of my mother, there is a square field	121
When I am buried in the village	125

*This Work Was Completed on December 1,
2010 at Italica Press, New York.
It Was Set in ITC Giovanni
and Herculanum and
Printed on 55-lb.
Natural Paper.*
❋ ❋

www.ingramcontent.com/pod-product-compliance
Lightning Source LLC
Chambersburg PA
CBHW031148160426
43193CB00008B/288